Modern Critical Interpretations

The Song of Songs

Modern Critical Interpretations

These and other titles in preparation

Modern Critical Interpretations

The Song of Songs

Edited and with an introduction by
Harold Bloom
Sterling Professor of the Humanities
Yale University

Chelsea House Publishers ◊ *1988*
NEW YORK ◊ NEW HAVEN ◊ PHILADELPHIA

© 1988 by Chelsea House Publishers, a division
of Chelsea House Educational Communications, Inc.

Introduction © 1988 by Harold Bloom

Printed and bound in the United States of America

10 9 8 7 6 5 4 3 2 1

∞ The paper used in this publication meets the minimum
requirements of the American National Standard for Permanence
of Paper for Printed Library Materials, Z39.48–1984.

Library of Congress Cataloging-in-Publication Data
The Song of songs / edited and with an introduction by Harold
Bloom.
    p.   cm.—(Modern critical interpretations)
  Bibliography: p.
  Includes index.
  ISBN 0–87754–917–6 (alk. paper) : $24.50
  1. Bible. O.T. Song of Solomon—Criticism, interpretation,
etc.
I. Bloom, Harold. II. Series.
BS1485.2.S66 1988
223′.9066—dc19   87–22181
                                      CIP

Contents

Editor's Note

This book brings together a representative selection of the best modern *literary* critical interpretations of the Song of Songs. The critical essays are reprinted here in the chronological order of their original publication. I am grateful to Kathleen Crozier for her aid in editing this volume.

My introduction briefly considers some of the possibilities for an intertextual reading of the Song. William E. Phipps begins the chronological sequence of criticism by pondering some of the unresolved paradoxes confronted by religious interpretations of the Song of Songs, while Marvin H. Pope meditates the ultimate paradox of the work, its bringing together, in strength, of love and death.

In Phyllis Trible's feminist reading, the Song, like the narrative of the Yahwist, redeems the Bible from much of its own male chauvinism and neglect of feminine perspectives. Marcia Falk centers upon the *Wasf,* an Arabic word for a poem that enumerates bodily images of the male and female, a genre that appears in the Bible only in the Song of Songs. Four difficult passages in the Song are expounded by Francis Landy, who shows how the difficulty enhances the Song's beauty.

Robert Alter reads the Song of Songs as a veritable garden of metaphor, surprisingly unlike most ancient Hebrew poetry in such reliance upon trope. This volume concludes with Arthur Green's fine exegesis of early Kabbalistic interpretations of the Song of Songs, interpretations that I think join the major poets influenced by the Song as the most fecund sources for new ways to read the Song of Songs.

Introduction

Rabbi Akiba, who is the dominant single figure in the entire history of normative Judaism, insisted upon bringing the Song of Songs into the canon of Scripture:

> The entire world is unworthy of the day the Song of Songs was given to Israel, for all of Scripture is holy, but the Song of Songs is the Holy of Holies.

Akiba is even reported to have said that the Song of Songs would have been sufficient to guide the world had Torah not been given. There is enough evidence of how Akiba interpreted the Song of Songs to suggest that he was the effectual originator of the immense history of allegorizing this poem or poems, though such allegorizing must have preceded him. The question of literal versus allegorical reading of the Song of Songs should be set aside forever; the work is so strong that it demands every mode that can be brought to it. My own emphasis here will be neither literal nor allegorical, but interpoetic. I cannot reread the Song of Songs without involuntarily rereading its greater poetic descendants, from the Kabbalists through Renaissance erotic lyricists on to Walt Whitman. To meditate upon the Song of Songs, for any reader conversant with Western imaginative traditions, is an activity that calls into play poems and prose by Isaac Luria and St. Teresa of Avila and St. John of the Cross, and by Fray Luis de León and Edmund Spenser, by Coventry Patmore and Walt Whitman, and many others.

The origins of the Song of Songs always may be in dispute, but my own ear for the Hebrew original tells me the work had one author, however many the redactors, and that she or he is unlike any other biblical poet. The notion, still held by some scholars, that we are reading a suite of folk songs is not worth arguing against; the sequence is as folksy and

1

simple as Ovid or Spenser or the young Shakespeare of *Venus and Adonis*. I also cannot take seriously the rival scholarly camp, which holds that the Song is cultic in character, reflecting the survival of pre-Judaic Canaanite fertility rituals. What I hear in the Song is a court poet, akin to the Spenser of the *Prothalamium* and the *Epithalamium,* a poet of enormous urbanity and cultivation, and of a highly sophisticated eroticism. I mean "court" in a very loose sense, and perhaps "aristocratic poet" would be a more useful phrase, since the likely date of composition is between the time of Ezra and Nehemiah and the Hellenistic period, with 400 B.C.E. a reasonable guess, making the Song roughly contemporary with that very different body of poetry, the Psalms.

Erotic poetry of such power and distinction must have stimulated normative misreadings almost from the start, and one sees how the interpretation of God as bridegroom and Israel as the beloved was inevitable. I do not believe that the poet of the Song had any intention of employing that prophetic trope, which had figured in Isaiah and even more strikingly in Jeremiah. The rabbis assimilated the Song to the prophets, an assimilation whose final consequence was the canonical passion of the great Akiba. Arthur Green, following Saul Lieberman, surmises that Akiba and his colleagues continued an esoteric tradition of interpreting the Song as commemorating the actual revelation of the body of God in the Sinai theophany. From this developed, centuries later, the grand Kabbalistic vision of the sexual union taking place within God, between God and the *Shekhinah,* the indwelling Sophia or wisdom-principle or female aspect of the Creator.

To this day, Kabbalistic interpretation seems to me the most fruitful of approaches to the Song of Songs, since it fuses the erotic and the spiritual, as the Song itself does, and since in essence it contains everything that is vital in an interpoetic or intrapoetic reading. Isaac Luria's Aramaic chant for the Sabbath joins itself to the Song of Songs by a great epiphany of God as bridegroom coming to embrace the Sabbath as his bride. God "enters the gates of the holy orchard of the apple trees" and "brings his Sabbath bride intense joy, in double measure, so that light and blessings pour upon her." In a related mode, St. Teresa of Avila celebrated her own union with God:

> By certain words that wound the soul who loves you, words
> scattered by you in the Canticles, and which you teach me to
> say to you! . . . My Lord, I ask nothing else in this life but
> "to kiss me with the kiss of Your mouth," and to do this in

such a manner that I should not be able to withdraw myself from this union, even if I wished it.

Closer even to the unique ethos of the Song of Songs are the *Ascent of Mount Carmel* and the *Living Flame of Love* of St. John of the Cross, each of them a commentary upon his ecstatic lyrics that recapture vital moments in the Song. It seems a strange path from the positive ecstasies of the Song to St. John's Dark Night of the Soul, but we will see the darkness that is there in the Song, and read the Song better, if we juxtapose to it:

4. This light guided me
   More surely than the light of noonday
   To the place where he (well I knew who!) was awaiting me—
   A place where none appeared.

5. Oh, night that guided me,
   Oh, night more lovely than the dawn,
   Oh, night that joined Beloved with lover,
   Lover transformed in the Beloved!

6. Upon my flowery breast,
   Kept wholly for himself alone,
   There he stayed sleeping, and I caressed him,
   And the fanning of the cedars made a breeze.

7. The breeze blew from the turret
   As I parted his locks;
   With his gentle hand he wounded my neck
   And caused all my senses to be suspended.

8. I remained, lost in oblivion;
   My face I reclined on the Beloved.
   All ceased and I abandoned myself,
   Leaving my cares forgotten among the lilies.

Luis de León, who was descended from a New Christian family of Jews who converted in 1492 so as not to suffer the Expulsion, and who brilliantly translated the Song into both verse and prose, is closer to the Song itself and to Kabbalistic tradition in always affirming his own identity even in the negative moment of union with the Divine. Willis Barnstone defends Luis de León from Spanish critics who see him as falling short of his contemporary mystic and poet, St. John of the Cross, since

Luis de León never allows himself to lose a sense of his own separate identity. I think Barnstone is right and that the Judaic element in Luis de León reminds us of the Song of Songs's own awareness that love unites only in act, not in essence. That may be why Spenser and Whitman seem to me closer to the Song of Songs than any other poets have been. Spenser's Puritanism, and Whitman's Hicksite Quaker heritage alike gave them a crucial consciousness of their own abiding individuality, and prevented them from totally losing themselves in visions of erotic union.

There is a final sense in which no poet has come close to a certain quality in the Song, to a terrible pathos that is unsurpassed in Western erotic literature:

> Set me as a seal upon thine heart, as a seal upon thine arm:
> for love is strong as death; jealousy is cruel as the grave: the
> coals thereof are coals of fire, which hath a most vehement
> flame.

The Hebrew is a little sharper than this, the unmatched King James version, since it calls love as fierce or intense as death or dying, and the Elizabethan "jealousy" is closer to "zealous" in its meaning. In the Hebrew, the poet chants that "passion is as strong as Sheol," or Hades, which affirms again the parallel intensities of loving and dying. The "coals of fire" are "darts of fire" in the Hebrew, and so confirm again the aggressive power of sexual love, so intimately related in the Song of Songs both to the death drive and to the transcendental possibilities of human existence.

The Plight of the Song of Songs

William E. Phipps

Over two millennia ago a member of the postexilic Jewish community wrote down some throbbing sentiments which he had heard sung about a couple in love. That anonymous editor's romantic bent is revealed in the superlative he used in the Hebrew title, *Shir ha-Shirim,* meaning the loveliest song. His disposition is also exposed in the dedication to Solomon, the greatest lover in the Israelite tradition—at least on a quantitative scale!

The Song of Songs is a song consisting of songs about intimate love. The editor probably contributed little to either the content or the organization of his collection. Like stringing a necklace, he loosely put together folk lyrics of varying lengths which added different facets of beauty to the unifying theme. He alternated frequently the male and female voices, but showed little concern for the sequence of ideas in arranging the stanzas.

The editor no doubt thought the meaning of his anthology would be transparently clear to readers. Even in his own day similar poems of the same genre were commonplace in the Near East from Egypt to Mesopotamia. What can be more easily understood universally than love's old sweet song? If John Milton is correct in assuming that simplicity and sensuousness are the basic ingredients of poetry in any language, the Song of Songs should not have caused difficult problems of interpretation.

It is one of the pranks of history that a poem so obviously about

From *Journal of the American Academy of Religion* 42, no. 1 (March 1974). © 1974 by the American Academy of Religion.

hungry passion has caused so much perplexity and has provoked such a plethora of bizarre interpretations. Even some contemporary scholars appear baffled by the Song of Songs. For example, T. J. Meek begins his commentary on the Song with this amazing and forbidding note: "Of all the books of the Old Testament none is so difficult to interpret." During the past century some scholars have claimed to have found in the Song the ritual chants used by those attempting to simulate the annual springtime marriage of a fertility god and goddess. But in the Hebrew culture sex had been demythologized: it was considered a proper sphere for man but not for deity. Others thought they had found in the Song a script intended for a theater production, complete with the chorus characteristic of Greek drama. Accordingly, a triangle was worked out, with a villainous Solomon and a virtuous shepherd vying for a rustic damsel. However, it takes much reading between the lines to find a plot, and there are no parallel extrabiblical dramas of the ancient Near East that might give such a conjecture plausibility.

There are several clues in ancient Jewish literature which suggest that the Song of Songs was originally a repertoire containing songs for members of wedding parties. First, we know that nuptial feasts lasted for several days and that role-playing as royalty was customary during that time. The *Mishnah* indicates that prior to the Roman destruction of Jerusalem the bridegroom wore a crown, possibly in imitation of King Solomon who was famous for attracting both wealth and women. Also, as Jeremiah shows, weddings were associated with mirthful music: "The voice of the bridegroom, the voice of the bride, the voices of those who sing."

It would be anachronistic to interpret the Song of Songs as infatuations and sexual experimentation of promiscuous youth. In the traditional Semitic culture marriage was covenanted near the age of puberty and intimate male-female association was not sanctioned prior to marriage. That the Song focuses on the betrothed or married couple is made explicit by the term *kallah,* meaning "spouse," which is frequently used in reference to the female partner. Coupled often with that term is *achoth* which literally means "sister." In the context of the Song it connotes psychophysical closeness rather than kinship. The idiom "my sister, my bride" could well be rendered "my dear wife."

The sexual innocence of the girl prior to matrimony is frequently alluded to in the Song of Songs by the tower and garden images. Parts of her body are compared to a high fortress that is able to withstand all who might try to destroy her defenses (4:4; 7:4; 8:10). Although she had previously remained inaccessible to all men, she now gladly opens up her virginal femininity to the great conqueror, her spouse. He commends her for having been "a garden locked, a fountain sealed" (4:12) and confesses that he has been looking forward to exploring the lush growth she has cultivated (7:8).

Interpreting the Song of Songs as lyrics principally used for wedding celebrations in lovely out-of-doors settings fits well into the Hebrew religious outlook. In that culture, unlike our own, it was not the unattached who were extolled by song. The first love song of the Bible depicts Adam rapturously exclaiming to his bride: "This at last is bone of my bones, and flesh of my flesh." In that Garden of Eden story, as in the Song of Songs, woman is of intrinsic value and no mention is made of her fecundity. Also, the sentiments of the couple in the Song who are "intoxicated with love" (5:1) are echoed in a poem from the book of Proverbs:

> Be grateful for your own fountain,
> And have your pleasure with the wife of your youth;
> A loveable doe! A sweet little mountain goat!
> May her breasts always intoxicate you!
> May you ever find rapture in loving her!
> (Proverbs 5:18–19, Anchor Bible)

The ancient Jews approved of physical passion between spouses since they believed that natural forces are a good creation of God. They thought that divine grandeur could be sensed through pleasant, as well as through painful, experiences. Some postbiblical Jewish sayings express well this point of view. An ancient rabbi commented: "A man will some day have to give an account to God for all the good things which his eyes beheld and of which he refused to enjoy." Robert Browning, after noting the psychosomatic holism of a distinguished medieval rabbi, wrote: "Let us cry, 'All good things / Are ours, nor soul helps flesh more, now, than flesh helps soul!'" Traditional values are also articulated in the prayer that concludes the Jewish wedding ceremony: "Blessed be thou, O Lord . . . who hast created joy and gladness, groom and bride, jubilation and exultation, pleasure and delight, love, brotherliness, peace and friendliness. . . . Blessed be thou, O Lord who makest rejoice the groom with his bride."

If sensuousness in male-female relationships was encouraged in the Song of Songs and in the Jewish community that interpreted it, why is it that for most of Judeo-Christian history this dominant motif of the Song has been muted, if not silenced altogether? To answer this question adequately, the principal concern of this essay, necessitates examining postbiblical Jewish and Christian treatments of the Song.

Dual Interpretations in Judaism

No reference is made to the Song of Songs in the earliest writings by Jews after the Old Testament era. It is not overtly alluded to in the writings of Philo, Josephus, or the New Testament. The first mention of the Song is in rabbinic literature and there it carries a double meaning. For example, in the *Mishnah* it is associated with the traditional wedding dance in which maidens participated. The "daughters of Jerusalem went forth to dance in the vineyard" and sang: "Young man, lift up your eyes and see whom you would choose for yourself." In addition to this literal interpretation, that rabbinic passage also places a symbolic meaning on sentiments from the Song. Solomon's wedding is interpreted to mean the giving of the Torah, and "the day of the gladness of his heart" (3:11) is taken to mean the building of the Temple.

Around 100 A.D. Akiba said: "He who sings the Song of Songs in wine taverns, treating it as if it were a vulgar song, forfeits his share in the world to come." What did he mean by that warning? Akiba held that "You shall love your neighbor as yourself" was the most fundamental truth in the Mosaic legislation. Assuming that he viewed one's spouse as at least as worthy as one's less intimate neighbor, the rabbi was concerned that the marital love expressed in the Song be given the dignity it deserved. Akiba and other rabbis thought of marriage as a *kiddushin,* meaning sanctification, so nuptial songs should not blaspheme the holy consummation. Far from being a bawdy song with only a secular significance, he boldly stated that it was the "holy of holies" of the sacred writings. He claimed that the Song had long been treasured by most members of the Jewish community.

There is no evidence that the ancient Jews rejected the literal sense of a writing either before or after accepting it as authoritative Scripture. The unadorned meaning remained prominent after canonization, even though speculations about additional theological and moral meanings were given. It was contrary to the respect which Jews gave to the plain meaning of their literature to accept only the allegorical meaning. Even Philo of Alexandria, who was the most allegorically prone of all Jews, did not discard its literal meaning. As regards Palestinian Judaism, R. P. C. Hanson has rightly observed: "Rabbinic allegory is characterized by the fact that it never for a moment impugns the validity of the literal sense."

The earliest Jewish commentary on the Song of Songs is in a targum dating from the sixth century A.D. Without denying the literal meaning, that commentary erects an allegorical superstructure over it. Following an analogy frequently found in the prophets, the groom symbolizes Yahweh and his bride is Judaism. A similar dual interpretation is later found in a commentary on the Song by Abraham ben Isaac in the fourteenth century. Israel Abrahams has stated that the Song was probably the most popular scriptural book for medieval Jews.

Greco-Christian Allegorization

Among Gentiles allegorization had a distinctly different purpose than it had in the Jewish community. Frequently Greek intellectuals, who found odious the obvious meaning of some poetry revered in their culture, substituted a basically opposing meaning to the objectionable lines. Allegorical interpretation can be traced to such early Greek philosophers as Xenophanes, Pythagoras, and Plato, who were offended by the alleged sexual activity and other anthropomorphic behavior of the Homeric gods.

The Stoics were the chief exponents of allegorism in the Hellenistic era. Believing that a man must be dispassionate to be truly moral, they were much embarrassed by the divine models of morality in Greek culture. By allegorizing the myths of gods who were thought to have been emotionally involved, the Stoics transposed the appearance of carnal passion into an acceptable discarnate spirituality.

In Christianity the Song of Songs received attention after the center of influence of the church moved from Jerusalem westward into the Greco-Roman social order. After the destruction of the Jewish state, the ethical standards affecting the church came more from Gentile than from Jewish culture. However, in pagan religion and philosophy it was commonplace to associate purity with sexual renunciation. Those Christians with a Roman background had come to respect the abstaining Vestal Virgins as exemplars of holy behavior. Also, in the Hellenistic cults of the Eastern Mediterranean, celibacy was associated with the sacred.

The generally contrasting outlook between Jews and Gentiles regarding sexuality precipitated a dilemma among Gentile Christians with respect to the Song of Songs. In the second century some of them rejected that book as an authoritative sacred writing. Marcion, for example, in part due to his zeal for sexual asceticism, advocated that Christians discard not only the Song but also the entire collection of Hebrew Scripture. None of those books belonged in the Christian canon, he believed, because they wrongly affirmed that the good God had created nature and natural impulses. However, Marcion's anti-Jewish position was too extreme for most Christians. Although they were uneasy about regarding the Song as sacrosanct, they realized that it would be easier to accept the entire Hebrew canon than to weigh individually whether or not each book was holy or profane. That procedure stifled dissent, but it left Christian interpreters with the acute embarrassment of having to explain a book that seemed to praise passionate sexual activity, which was generally believed to be the root of much evil.

Allegory was brought to the rescue. Having noticed the effective way in which the philosophers had recast the sensuous gods of Homer and Hesiod into ethereal ideals, Christian theologians were quick to interpret the sensuous celebration by a couple in Song of Songs as a non-physical prayer communion between a pious Christian and his ever-loving God. Thus the passionate paean which the church had inherited from the authoritative books of the synagogue was converted into what was thought to be a harmless mysticism. Indeed, it came to be reckoned as one of the most important books by sexually ascetic Christians, because allegorical sermons on it showed how the dishonorable libidinous drives could be pommelled and sublimated. Jean Leclercq, an authority on monasticism, has called the Song "the book which was most read and most frequently commented on in the medieval cloister." From the third century until the nineteenth, Christian interpreters have usually treated the Song as an allegory, with each finding hidden beneath the sexual imagery his preconceived Christological and ascetic doctrines.

Hippolytus, a Roman who flourished around 200 A.D., is the first Christian on record to have allegorized the Song of Songs. The fragments of his commentary that remain show that he transformed the Song into a vehicle for conveying an austere ethic. Those who crucify their fleshly desires are elevated to the "hill of frankincense" (4:6). "The king has brought me into his chambers" (1:4) is interpreted to mean that Jesus has brought Christians to whom he is wedded into the church. Switching his symbolism, Hippolytus has Christians sucking from the bride's two breasts (4:5), which represent the Old and New Covenants.

Origen, a younger contemporary of Hippolytus, may have been influenced by the earlier allegorist. Both shared the conviction that the caressing king connotes Jesus, and his bride represents either the corporate church or the individual Christian. Origen composed sermons and a ten-volume commentary on the Song of Songs which is only in small part extant. In the prologue to the commentary he warned passionate persons not to read further. He regarded the Song as safe reading only for older persons who are no longer troubled by sexual desires. In the prologue to his commentary he stated: "Everyone who is not yet rid of the vexations of flesh and blood and has not ceased to feel the passion of his bodily nature should refrain completely from reading this book."

Those words display Origen's proneness toward extremism. When he was young he took too literally Jesus' hyperbole about cutting off bodily members that cause one to sin, and thus he castrated himself. Later in life he took too figuratively the Song of Songs and rejected its literal meaning. Eunuch Origen was sure that God never intended the book to be understood except as a purely spiritual drama of the inner life. The dark bride (1:8) represents the Christian whose stain of carnal sin has not been washed away. Her desire for the groom's left hand under her head while being fondled by his right hand (2:6) means that the church longs for the glory and eternity of Jesus. These are samples of the way in which Origen ingeniously denatured the sexual sentiments of the Song. In the course of his writing he made this plea: "We earnestly beg the hearers of these things to mortify their carnal senses. They must not take anything of what has been said with reference to bodily functions but rather employ them for grasping those divine senses of the inner man" (*Commentary on the Song of Songs*).

Origen introduced Plato's interpretation of love into Christianity by means of his Song of Songs allegory. Plato had distinguished between opposing earthly and heavenly loves. The former was associated with the sensual and the latter with the superior nonphysical sphere. Origen wrote in a Platonic manner: "There is a love of the flesh which comes from Satan, and there is also another love, belonging to the Spirit, which has its origin in God; and nobody can be possessed by the two loves. . . . If you have despised all bodily things . . . then you can acquire spiritual love" (*Homilies on the Song of Songs*).

The sacred marriage mystery of Hellenistic religions was of even more immediate influence upon Origen than Plato's theory of love. Adolf Harnack has pointed out that Origen was indebted to those pagan Gnostics who treated the divine Spirit as the exclusive bridegroom of the devotee.

The *Acts of Thomas,* which reflects Gnostic currents of Origen's day, affords an excellent illustration of the heavenly union that is claimed by those who shun fleshly entanglements. In one episode an earthly wedding becomes the setting for the renunciation of sexual intercourse. According to that apocryphal Gospel, a divine epiphany followed a wedding prayer given by the apostle Thomas. Jesus appeared and proclaimed: "If you abandon this filthy intercourse you become holy temples, pure and free from afflictions and pains both manifest and hidden, and you will not be girt about with cares for life and for children, the end of which is destruction." Consequently, that night the terrified couple "refrained from the filthy passion" and afterward the bride claimed: "I have set at naught this man and this marriage which passes away from before my eyes, because I am bound in another marriage. I have had no intercourse with a short-lived husband . . . because I am yoked with the true man." In another story the identity of the immortal bridegroom is made explicit. Thomas advised another wife to abstain from "horrid intercourse" for it leads to "eternal damnation." Accepting his advice, she repelled the sexual advances of a kind husband with these contemptuous words: "He whom I love is better than you and your possessions. . . . Jesus himself will set me free from the shameful deeds which I did with you. . . . You are a bridegroom who passes away and is destroyed, but Jesus is a true bridegroom, abiding immortal for ever."

In the fourth century, when monasticism was undergoing rapid development, the ideas of nonsexual sacred marriage which Origen imported from pagan Hellenism became enormously popular. This is displayed in a preface written by Jerome for a translation of Origen's sermons on the Song of Songs. That Latin scholar wrote: "While Origen surpassed all writers in his other books, in his Song of Songs he surpassed himself." The Song was viewed by Jerome as a poem praising virgins who mortify the flesh. He informed them that Jesus would titillate those who detest physical relationships with other men: "Ever let the Bridegroom fondle you. . . . He will put his hand through the opening and will touch your body. And you will arise trembling and cry, 'I am lovesick.'" While Jerome polemicized against coitus on the physical level, he was engrossed in it on a fantasy level.

Aware that a novice might miss what he saw in the Song of Songs, Jerome prescribed that a girl should not study the book until other studies were completed. "If she were to read it at the beginning," he asserted, "she might be harmed by not perceiving that it was the song of a spiritual wedding expressed in fleshly language." In accordance with his motto, *omnis coitus impurus,* Jerome assured those who withstood sexual defilement until death that they would be rewarded by Jesus their bridegroom. He will say to each one to whom he is married who is resting in a grave:

"Rise up, my fair one, my dove, and come; for lo, the winter is past, the rain is over and gone." By inverted interpretations such as this, monk Jerome took the book of Scriptures that posed the greatest threat to sexual asceticism and converted it into an asset.

Gregory of Nyssa, a prominent Greek bishop, allegorized the Song of Songs in his fifteen sermons on that book. He praised Origen's treatment of the Song from the previous century. Accordingly, he informed those who interpret it literally that they are obscene and will be punished in hell. The entire book, according to Gregory, deals exclusively with an exchange between the soul and God. But only when the soul becomes passionless can it become fully united with God. Gregory shows his Platonism in such affirmations as these: "The love of God can only arise from what is contrary to carnal desire" and "The life of flesh and blood must be mortified by the contemplation of spiritual reality." The bride's testimony, "I slept but my heart was awake" (5:2), is interpreted to mean: "The soul, enjoying alone the contemplation of Being, will not awake for anything that arouses sensual pleasure. After lulling to sleep every bodily motion, it receives the vision of God in a divine wakefulness with pure and naked intuition."

Ambrose, a contemporary of Jerome and Gregory, also found in the Song of Songs a vivid account of the Christian who turns away from the pleasures of the flesh in order to sport with Jesus. Accordingly, "O that you would kiss me!" (1:2) refers to the Lord's faithful who had long waited for his coming with ardent hope. After his incarnation, this invitation was extended: "Come with me from Lebanon" (4:8). To accept Jesus' call, Ambrose contended, involves renouncing the world and concentrating all affections on him. It is the virgins who are properly prepared for their heavenly spouse. "My breasts were like towers" (8:10) refers to those whose sexual organs are impregnable and thereby "with unspotted chastity keep the couch of the Lord holy." The devout are invited to the Eucharist where they can "eat, drink, and be inebriated" (5:1). Ambrose also finds in the Song references to the mother of Jesus. For example, "I am a rose of Sharon" (2:1) is taken to be Jesus' claim that he budded forth from a virgin's womb.

Bernard of Clairvaux, the towering church leader of the twelfth century, is principally known as a writer by his allegorical interpretation of the Song of Songs. He prepared eighty-six sermons on that book, averaging more than two sermons per verse for the first two chapters completed! Like the medieval alchemist, he was obsessed with desire to transform material which he regarded as base into something precious.

He had contempt for the flesh and females and was determined to show that the life of the spirit was unalloyed with sex. He followed previous Christian allegorists in thinking that only a vile person would interpret the Song as an expression of natural feelings. He urged: "Take heed that you bring chaste ears to this discourse of love; and when you think of these two lovers, remember always that not a man and a woman are to be thought of, but the Word of God and a Soul." Thus he viewed the love song as a mystic cryptogram which is unlocked by reading as Orphic literature. The bride's boast, "I am black but beautiful" (1:5), is interpreted to portray the contrast between the ugliness of the soul in the present corporeal entombment and the luster it will have when it wings away into eternity. "I sought him, but found him not" (3:1) means, according to Bernard, that our not finding God is due to our being "imprisoned in the flesh, sunk in mire."

As with other allegorists, Bernard's alleged exposition tells us nothing about the scriptural text, but rather exposes the turmoil of the mystic composer. One of his contemporaries relates a telling episode from the life of Bernard that shows his dread of sex. During his youth an exchange of admiring glances with a girl triggered an erection. Because he associated sensual passion with the fire of hell, he plunged into a pond of icy water to extinguish his burning concupiscence. When his tumescence subsided, he resolved that he would become a celibate.

"If you drive nature out with a pitchfork," Horace sagiously observed, "she will find a way back." Bernard's repressed erotic urges resulted in a destructive flood of dark passion in later life. By means of an inverted sublimation, he channeled his ardent desire for the opposite sex into a hatred of alleged heretics and infidels. In particular he had an antipathy toward Peter Abelard which was in large part due to a different assessment of human love. Abelard believed that natural urges were not sinful due to having inherited contaminated sexuality from Adam's fall. He inquired: "If cohabitation with a wife and the enjoyment of pleasant things were allowed us in Paradise from the first day of our creation without guilt being incurred, who may argue that these things are now sinful, provided only that we do not exceed the limits of our permission?"

Bernard was outraged by Abelard's criticism of the Augustinian doctrine of original sin. Consequently, he requested Pope Innocent to exterminate the "fox destroying the Lord's vineyard." Appropriating imagery from the Song of Songs in reference to anyone who deviated from the prevailing outlook of the church was probably suggested to Bernard by his mentor Augustine. That Bishop of Hippo had interpreted

"Your teeth are like a flock of shore ewes" (4:2) as an allusion to the teeth of saints tearing at heretics! He confessed that it gave him pleasure to envisage Christians as "cutting off men from their errors and transferring them to the church after their hardness has been softened as if by being bitten and chewed."

As a result of Bernard's efforts, Abelard was excommunicated and his books were burned. It is unlikely that Bernard was satisfied with this punishment, for he proclaimed in a Song of Songs sermon that "heretics should be put to death." Peter the Venerable, who lamented Bernard's self-appointed role as heresy hunter, wrote him these candid words: "You perform all the difficult religious duties; you fast, you watch, you suffer; but you will not endure the easy ones—you do not love." Arthur C. McGiffert points even more acutely to the irony of Bernard's character: "For all his praise of love he was a violent hater."

Bernard used his sermons on the Song of Songs to chastise his enemies outside the church as well as within. He thought it was a Christian's duty to despise those assumed to be rejected by God. With regard to a person who is commonly recognized as an enemy, he asserted: "It is necessary that you think of him not as almost nothing but as nothing at all." Consequently, Bernard wrote numerous letters to influential Europeans urging that the Moslems in Palestine be altogether crushed. In one he exclaimed:

> What multitudes of sinners, confessing their offences with sorrow, have in that Holy Land been reconciled to God, since the swords of Christian warriors drove thence the foul pagans!
> . . . The Living God has charged me to proclaim that he will take vengeance upon such as refuse to defend him against his foes. To arms, then! Let a holy indignation animate you to the combat, and let the cry of Jeremiah reverberate through Christendom: "Cursed be he that withholdeth his sword from blood."
>
> ("Letter to the Bavarians")

Captivated by Bernard's ascetic appearance and fiery rhetoric, thousands joined to form the Second Crusade. At Chartres he was chosen as its commander-in-chief, but because of his age he declined the honor.

It has been recognized that devotion to aggressive war becomes for some persons a substitute for frustrated love. Bernard provides an excellent case study of one who substituted the arrows of Mars for the darts of Cupid. "Make war, not love" might have been an appropriate slogan for that saint!

Strangely enough, Bernard has been singled out by some as one of the most Christlike persons in church history. In his own era Dante regarded him as the supreme guide to the heavenly realm. A Protestant theologian of the present century concluded his lengthy study of Bernard with this not atypical evaluation: "One does not know where else to look for a more lofty and shining exhibition of the power of faith." If Bernard exemplified what has been recently called the golden age of Western spirituality, it is indeed a sad commentary on the course of Christianity.

In late medieval Catholicism, allegorical interpretations of the Song of Songs were popular among both the unscholarly mystics and the philosophical theologians. The writings of celibate Jan van Ruysbroek are an example of the former. The Song was a main source of his imagery for expressing the delectable climax of the soul's intercourse with the Divine Bridegroom. Thomas Aquinas exemplifies scholasticism's appreciation of the Song in that it provided the text for his last sermon before death. A medieval hagiographer tells of that event in this way: "It was indeed appropriate that the great worker in the school of the Church should terminate his teaching on that song of eternal glory; that such a master in that school, when about to pass from the prison of the body to the heavenly wedding feast, should discourse on that bridal union of the Church with Christ her spouse."

The Song of Songs has continued to be principally interpreted as an allegory in the modern history of Roman Catholicism. In the Douay version, which has served for several centuries as the approved English translation for Catholics, there is an unusual treatment of one verse of the Song. Following the Vulgate's mistranslation, the bridegroom's words read:

> Under the apple tree I raised thee up:
> There thy mother was corrupted,
> There she was deflowered that bore thee.
> (8:5)

Jerome, who regarded even marital sexuality defiling, read his own ascetic bias into his Latin translation. To compound that inaccuracy, the Douay Bible added this Christological annotation: "*Under the apple tree I raised thee up; that is that Christ redeemed the Gentiles at the foot of the cross, where the synagogue of the Jews (the mother church) was corrupted* by their denying him, and crucifying him." However, the Hebrew and Septuagint texts should be translated thus:

> Under the fruit trees I roused you:
> There your mother brought you forth,
> There she who bore you was in labor.

During the past decade there has been a recognition by some Catholic exegetes that the Song of Songs was originally intended to be understood as lyrics of human lovers and should now be interpreted as such. However, *The Jerusalem Bible* and *A New Catholic Commentary* display that most Roman Catholic interpreters today retain an allegorical interpretation. In the former tome, for example, Jesus is found hidden in the image of the bride's "brother" (8:1) and Mary's Immaculate Conception is discovered in the description of the bride as "unblemished" (4:7). That Marian doctrine implies that ordinary mortal conception is soiled with sin, so a bias against sex has not yet been purged from the Catholic interpretation of the Song.

Protestant scholars, until the past century, also generally upheld an allegorical interpretation of the Song of Songs. Luther was inconsistent in this regard. On the one hand he expressed himself in this manner: "So far as allegories are concerned Origen is a prince, a king; he filled the whole Bible with secret interpretations of this kind, which aren't worth a damn. The reason was that they all followed their own conceits, thoughts and opinions, as they thought fit." However, Luther inconsistently criticized any who might be tempted to interpret the Song literally and could not resist imposing on it his political bent. Offering a unique interpretation, he claimed that the book was written to encourage peasants to be obedient to their divinely ordained rulers. Hence, "Stir not up nor awaken love" (8:4) means: "You cities, whoever you are under this worship and government of God, take care to be quiet and peaceful, lest you incite disturbance."

English Protestants have been influenced for several centuries by the headings provided by the translators of the King James version of the Bible. For example, "The church having a taste of Christ's love" is the interpretive clue given for these sentiments by the bride: "My beloved put in his hand by the hole of the door, and my bowels were moved for him" (5:4). Christ affectionately reciprocates with imagery such as this: "The joints of thy thighs are like jewels. . . . Thy navel is like a round goblet, which wanteth not liquor" (7:1–2). The church's prayer for Christ's second coming is found in this verse: "Make haste, my beloved;

and be thou like to a roe or to a young hart upon the mountains of spices" (8:14).

Presbyterians and Methodists have been warned by high authority to avoid the plain meaning of the Song of Songs. In the seventeenth century the Westminster Assembly censured interpreters who have blasphemously "received it as a hot carnall pamphlet formed by some loose Apollo or Cupid." John Wesley informed his followers:

> The description of this bridegroom and bride is such as could not with decency be used or meant concerning Solomon and Pharoah's daughter; that many expressions and descriptions, if applied to them, would be absurd and monstrous; and that it therefore follows that this book is to be understood allegorically concerning that spiritual love and marriage which is between Christ and his church.
>
> (*Explanatory Notes upon the Old Testament*)

A SONG OF HUMAN LOVE

Throughout most of the history of the church it has been regarded as false and morally pernicious to interpret the Song of Songs literally. However, around 400 A.D., there was one clergyman in the Latin church and one in the Greek church who advocated that the plain meaning of the Song be respected. In Rome, during the heyday of sexual asceticism, Jovinian urged that the marital state not be denigrated by commending those who make vows of perpetual virginity as having the morally superior life style. He appealed to Scripture to show that the married were not, in the sight of God, inferior to the virgins. In particular he claimed that the Song is full of the idea that marital sexuality is hallowed.

Latin prelates were incensed by Jovinian's position, for they saw it as subversive to the monastic movement that they ardently supported. Consequently Jerome, in a long diatribe, attacked both Jovinian and the sanctity of marriage. He used allegorical counterfeit in an attempt to reject Jovinian's appeal to the Song of Songs as evidence that sexual expression can be as holy as repression. Jerome held that the true meaning of the Song is diametrically opposite to the literal meaning—the book is designed to teach that sexual abstinence is the way to avoid sin. Bishop Ambrose and Pope Siricius joined Jerome in condemning Jovinian for "heresy" and "blasphemy" at council meetings in Milan and Rome. Ambrose, who had allegorized the Song to embroider his sexual asceticism, found Jovinian's biblical interpretation hideous. Siricius, who referred to marital sexuality of those in holy orders as "obscene cupidity," was likewise disposed to reject Jovinian's assessment of sexuality.

In the Eastern church, Theodore of Mopsuestia protested the allegorization of Scripture because it perverted its plain meaning. In particular, that bishop asserted that the Song of Songs was a love song in which Solomon celebrated his marriage with an Egyptian bride. Doubtless his mode of interpretation was influenced by his belief that sexual desire was not inherently impure. His openness to the positive values of sexuality is evidenced in his belief that even the sinless Jesus had fleshly impulses. Theodore's position was too radical for his ascetic milieu. Even his student, Bishop Theodoret, declared that Theodore's interpretation of the Song was "not even fitting in the mouth of a crazy woman." A century later, in 553, the Council of Constantinople condemned Theodore's interpretation and anathematized the bishop. Understandably there were for the next millennium no other churchmen brazen enough to defend interpreting the Song as passionate love poetry about a man and a maiden.

It was not until John Calvin rejected the allegorical mode of interpretation that scholars began to reappraise the Song of Songs. That sixteenth-century Reformer forthrightly stated his position in this way:

> Origen, and many others along with him, have seized the occasion of torturing Scripture, in every possible manner, away from the true sense. They concluded that the literal sense is too mean and poor, and that, under the outer bark of the letter, there lurk deeper mysteries, which cannot be extracted but by beating out allegories. . . . [But] the true meaning of Scripture is the natural and obvious meaning.
> *(Commentaries on Galatians and Ephesians)*

Sebastian Castellio, who studied under Calvin, was convinced that the Song of Songs should be understood literally, but he was not convinced that it was worthy to stand in the canon of Holy Scripture. He is reported to have called it "a lascivious and obscene poem in which Solomon described his indecent amours." Calvin strongly disagreed with Castellio's moral judgment on this matter, and this can be attributed to their different attitudes toward sexuality. Calvin, in his exposition of 1 Corinthians 7 stated: "Conjugal intercourse is a thing that is pure, honorable, and holy." Accordingly, he held that the Song was an unsullied nuptial ode similar to Psalm 45. In both, Calvin argued, Solomon sings of the beauty of the Creator's handicraft and so it is presumptuous for anyone to reject what has been declared good by God. Calvin also saw in those historical wedding lyrics a premonition of the quality of love that later would form a convenantal bond between Christ and his church. He did not think it improper to associate the marriage bed celebration with the deepest divine manifestation of love. So rather than banishing the Song from the inspired canon, Calvin used his influence to deny ordination to Castellio and expel him from his teaching position in Geneva.

Castellio's outlook made sense to those who placed negative valuation on both allegorical and sexual expression. An example of this attitude is found in the eighteenth-century scholar William Whiston, who held that the Song of Songs is filled with earthy erotic exchanges and that therefore it is altogether out of place in a collection of sacred literature.

Edmund Spenser, an English Puritan, seems to have been the first scholar to accept Calvin's position that the Song of Songs is both divinely inspired and a song of human love. He translated the book and alluded to it frequently in his poems. The Song is especially prominent in the lovely poem which he composed in 1594 to commemorate his own wedding. When making an inventory of female features, the Song provided the source for some of his images. Thus Spenser describes his "truest, turtle dove" in this way:

> Her goodly eyes lyke saphyres shining bright,
> Her forehead yvory white,
> Her cheekes lyke apples which the sun hath rudded,
> Her lips lyke cherryes charming men to byte,
> Her brest like to a bowle of creame uncrudded,
> Her paps lyke lyllies budded,
> Her snowie necke lyke to a marble towre,
> And all her body like a pallace fayre,
> Ascending uppe with many a stately stayre,
> To honors seat and chastities sweet bowre.
> ("Epithalamion")

Having disciplined his desires for some forty years as a bachelor, Spenser looked forward to his wedding as a consecrated consummation:

> Never had man more joyfull day then this,
> . . . .
> This day for ever to me holy is.

It was not until two centuries after Spenser that a commentary was produced in which the Song of Songs was interpreted as a charming expression of natural love that points to the holiness of human relations. This was accomplished by Johann G. von Herder, a leader in eighteenth-century German Romanticism, who was attracted to poetry in which the divine is enmeshed with nature and human feelings. He found in the Song a sequence of independent ditties extolling sentimental and physical love as pure. Due in large part to Herder's influence on Johann W. von Goethe's education, that poet came to have appreciation for the beauty of unembellished nature. Goethe showed the influence of his mentor when he claimed that the Song is "the most tender and inimitable expression of graceful yet passionate love that has come down to us. . . . The principal theme is an ardent longing of youthful hearts, seeking, finding, repulsing, attracting, under various most simple conditions."

In the centuries since Herder a number of novel interpretations of the Song of Songs have been advanced, but few have been convinced by them. The most scholarly review of these modern interpretations has been given by H. H. Rowley. He concludes with a judgment that is essentially the same as that of Theodore, Jovinian, Calvin, Spenser, and Herder: "The view I adopt finds in it nothing but what it appears to be, lovers' songs, expressing their delight in one another and the warm emotion of their hearts. All of the other views find in the Song what they bring to it." Rowley thinks that the Song deserves to be included in the authoritative literature of the Christian religion even though it is a duet of an erotic couple. He comments: "The Church has always consecrated the union of man and woman in matrimony, and taught that marriage is a divine ordinance, and it is not unfitting that a book which expresses the spiritual and physical emotions on which matrimony rests should be given a place in the canon of Scripture."

CONCLUSION

"There is no instinct that has been so maligned, suppressed, abused, and distorted by religious teaching as the instinct of sex." This observation of Dora (Mrs. Bertrand) Russell has been amply confirmed by the hermeneutical history of the Song of Songs. However, she is indiscriminate in criticizing religious teaching generally for mistreatment of sexuality. Judaism has from the beginning been distinctively different from those religions which give the impression that coitus is at best a lamentable necessity for human survival. Jewish novelist Herman Wouk has rightly discerned that the Western notion that sexual intercourse is somehow wrong "is the ghost of crushed paganism rising out of the marble of overthrown temples to Venus in the walls and floors of early Christian churches."

With respect to the Song of Songs, Theodore of Mopsuestia was the only church leader of stature during Christianity's first 1,500 years who appreciated the original meaning of the Song and had the courage to go against the strong currents of sexual asceticism of his culture in defending his position. Although he was condemned as a heretic, respect for his hermeneutics is now increasing. McGiffert has justifiably called him "the greatest exegete of the ancient church."

Interpreting the Song of Songs as lyrics of human love has confronted prelates with an embarrassing dilemma. If, on the one hand, the book's prima facie meaning was acknowledged, then the established assumption about the superiority of those persons in the church devoted to lifelong sexual abstinence is called into question. On the other hand, if the book was renounced, what would prohibit Christians from calling into question other biblical books which had been appealed to as authoritative? Given these practical problems, it is easy to understand why allegory was brought to the rescue even though there is no clue within the Song to suggest that it was originally composed with another meaning in mind. Polonius's wry words are germane: "Though this be madness, yet there is method in it."

Allegorists were able to do much more than uphold the dogma of inspiration of all alleged "Holy Scriptures" and the doctrine that fleshly indulgence is morally inferior to marital renunciation. They were able to cull phrases from the Song of Songs that could communicate an ego-satisfying private mysticism that had been imported from Greek religion. Orphism, which was transmitted by Pythagoreanism, Platonism, and Stoicism into Gentile Christianity, emphasized that those who rigorously subdued their emotions would be rewarded by suprarational ecstasy and by union of their souls with the ultimate Spirit. Even though the notion of solitary salvation was foreign to the dominant thrust of biblical religion, allegorists realized that symbols from the Song could be appropriated for the ethereal "flight of the alone to the Alone."

The defect of most Christian allegorical interpretations is not that they find heavenly overtones in the language of lovers, but that they find little or no religious significance in natural beauty, emotional feeling, and physical relations. Although God is not mentioned in the Song, there is in the book an implicit praise to the One who has created the exquisite handiwork of the out-of-doors and has encouraged his creatures to enjoy spontaneous wooing. For the prominent Christian allegorists, it was unthinkable that honeymoon caressing could be hallowed. As moral dualists there could be for them no traffic between sensuous contact and spiritual union. Love of God was antithetical to sexual love. Such a doctrine cannot be legitimately grounded in any of the Judaeo-Christian Scriptures.

When Lutheran pastor Dietrich Bonhoeffer was engaged to be married, he related this experience to the Song of Songs. Before his martyrdom in a Nazi prison he grandly affirmed:

> God requires that we should love him eternally with our whole hearts, yet not so as to compromise or diminish our earthly affections, but as a kind of *cantus firmus* to which the other melodies of life provide the counterpoint. Earthly affection is one of these contrapuntal themes, a theme which enjoys an autonomy of its own. Even the Bible can find room for the Song of Songs, and one could hardly have a more passionate and sensual love than is there portrayed (see 7:6). It is a good thing that that book is included in the Bible as a protest against those who believe that Christianity stands for restraint of passion.
>
> *(Letters and Papers from Prison)*

These sentiments display Bonhoeffer's conviction that Christians have erred in reading the "New Testament far too little on the basis of the Old." He was aware that the God of Israel was the "beyond" in the midst of our human loves.

The most sensuous book in Scripture and in all the writings of antiquity is the Song of Songs. As a book of religion it is at least as sublime as a number of other biblical books. It tells of the joyfulness and constancy of genuine affection. It glorifies a bond that is sweeter than honey and stronger than a lion. The affirmation "Love is strong as death" (8:6) is excelled only by the New Testament proclamation that love is even stronger than death.

Interpretations of the Sublime Song: Love and Death

Marvin H. Pope

It has been recognized by many commentators that the setting of Love and Passion in opposition to the power of Death and Hell in 8:6c,d is the climax of the Canticle and the burden of its message: that Love is the only power that can cope with Death. Throughout the Song the joys of physical love are asserted, but this singular mention of Death and his domain, Sheol, suggests that this fear may be the covert concern of the Canticle, the response to inexorable human fate with the assertion of Love as the only power that frustrates the complete victory of Death. The sacred marriage was a celebration and affirmation of this vital force. The inevitable circumstance in which Life and Love come into stark confrontation with Death is in mortuary observances, not only in the wake and burial but in the ongoing concern to commune with the departed and provide for their needs in the infernal realm with offerings of food and drink.

The sacral meal with ritual drinking of intoxicating beverage, music, song, dance, and sexual license was a feature of religious praxis in the Near East from early times. Glyptic art of ancient Mesopotamia presents vivid scenes of such festivities. Seals from the Royal Cemetery at Ur depict banquet scenes with celebrants imbibing from large jars through drinking tubes while a bed with cross bands is presented by an attendant. The cross bands, or saltire, are the symbol and attribute of the great goddess of love and war. The saltire of the love goddess adorning the couch (perhaps also serving to brace it) suggests the use to which it will

From *The Anchor Bible: The Song of Songs: A New Translation with Introduction and Commentary.* © 1977 by Doubleday Dell Publishing Group, Inc.

shortly be put and this is graphically confirmed in other scenes which show the bed occupied by a copulating couple. Beneath the love couch is sometimes depicted the scorpion, symbol of the goddess Išhara, or the dog related to the goddess Gula. Both these goddesses, Išhara and Gula, are, according to H. Frankfort, "aspects of that great goddess of fertility whose union with a male god, consummated at the New Year's festival, insured the prosperity of the community; for the fertility of nature depended upon this act." The dog under the love couch depicted on a Mesopotamian seal of the Early Dynastic III period (ca. 2500 B.C.), see figure 1, recalls the canine beneath the couch which is common on Hellenistic funerary sculptures but which has not been plausibly explained. A recently published Ugaritic text, however, when correlated with observations by a couple of Fathers of the Church concerning accusations against the early Christians, throws light on the persistent canine at the connubium and the funeral feast. The Ugaritic text UG 5.1 describes a banquet given by El, the father of the gods, in which a dog has an important but unspecified role. The highlights of the affair are given here in translation without notes.

El offered game in his house,
Venison in the midst of his palace.
He invited the gods to mess.
The gods ate and drank,
Drank wine till sated,
Must till inebriated.

. . . .

. . . .

'Astarte and Anat arrived
'Astarte prepared a *brisket* for him,
And Anat a shoulder.
The Porter of El's house chided them:
"Lo, for the dog prepare a *brisket,*
For the cur prepare a shoulder."
El his father he chided.
El sat (in) (his pl)ace,
El sat in his *mrzḥ.*
He drank wine till sated,
Must till inebriated.

. . . .

. . . .

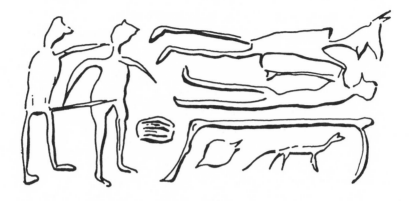

Figure 1. Early Mesopotamian "sacred marriage" scene with dog under the couch

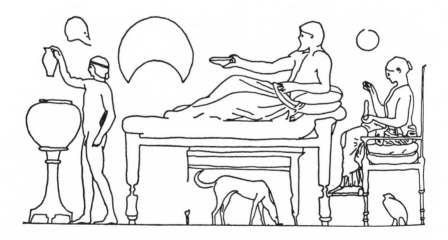

Figure 2. Anatolian tomb relief

An apparition accosted him,
With horns and a tail.
He floundered in his excrement and urine.
El collapsed, El like those who descend into Earth.
Anat and 'Astarte went roaming.

There is a gap of a couple of lines on the obverse of the tablet and the text continues for several lines on the reverse, with mention of the return of the goddesses and the administration of various medicines, including juice of green olives, to relieve the deity's crapulence.

The mention of special pieces of meat for the dog, the same cuts prepared by the goddesses for their father, recalls the allegations against the early Christians regarding the role of the dog in their festal meals. Tertullian in chapters 7 and 8 of his *Apology* (ca. 197) in rebutting the charges that Christians in their reprobate feasts murdered and ate infants and climaxed the celebration with an incestuous sexual orgy, mentions dogs as "the pimps of darkness" procuring license for these impious lusts by putting out the lights in a rather bizarre fashion. Tertullian ridiculed the charges simply by recounting the alleged proceedings:

> Yet, I suppose, it is customary for those who wish to be initiated to approach first the father of the sacred rites to arrange what must be prepared. . . . Now, you need a baby, still tender, one who does not know what death means, and who will smile under your knife. You need bread, too, with which to gather up his juicy blood; besides that, candlesticks, lamps, some dogs and bits of meat which will draw them on to overturn the lamps. Most important of all, you must come with your mother and sister.
>
> (*Apology*)

These rites were alleged to have been performed for the purpose of gaining eternal life, to which charge Tertullian retorted:

> For the time being, believe it! On this point I have a question to ask: If you believed it, would you consider the acquisition of eternal life worth attaining with such a (troubled) conscience? Come, bury your sword in this baby, enemy though he be of no one, guilty of no crime, everybody's son; or, if that is the other fellow's job, stand here beside this (bit of) humanity, dying before he has lived; wait for the young soul to take flight; receive his fresh blood; saturate your bread with

it; partake freely! Meanwhile, as you recline at table, note the place where your mother is, and your sister; note it carefully, so that, when the dogs cause the darkness to fall, you may make no mistake—for you will be guilty of a crime unless you commit incest.

(Apology)

Marcus Minucius Felix (fl. 200–240) tells us a bit more about these alleged initiation rites for Christian novices:

An infant covered with a dough crust to deceive the unsuspecting is placed beside the person to be initiated into the sacred rites. This infant is killed at the hands of the novice by wounds inflicted unintentionally and hidden from his eyes, since he has been urged on as if to harmless blows on the surface of the dough. The infant's blood—oh, horrible—they sip up eagerly; its limbs they tear to pieces, trying to outdo each other; by this victim they are leagued together; by being privy to this crime they pledge themselves to mutual silence. These sacred rites are more shocking than any sacrilege.

(Octavius)

Minucius Felix continues:

On the appointed day, they assemble for their banquets with all their children, sisters, and mothers—people of both sexes and every age. After many sumptuous dishes, when the company at the table has grown warm and the passion of incestuous lust has been fired by drunkenness, a dog which has been tied to a lampstand is tempted by throwing a morsel beyond length of the leash by which it is bound. It makes a dash, and jumps for the catch. Thus, when the witnessing light has been overturned and extinguished, in the ensuing darkness which favors shamelessness, they unite in whatever revolting lustful embraces the hazard of chance will permit. Thus, they are all equally guilty of incest, if not in deed, yet by privity, since whatever can happen in the actions of individuals is sought for by the general desire of all.

(Octavius)

Dogs figure in cultic symbolism and funerary rites of many cultures and there is no warrant to consider the topic in detail here since dogs play no part in the Song of Songs. The practice of putting pieces of meat on or around a corpse, as among the Parsees is easily understood as intended to distract the dogs from attacking the corpse. There is a rabbinic story about the death of King David and the cutting of an animal's carcass to keep the hungry dogs from attacking the corpse. Other references to food for dogs at funerals and weddings occur in rabbinic literature. An Anatolian funerary relief from Thasos, dating to the fifth century B.C., shows a dog under the banquet couch with muzzle to the ground, as if eating (figure 2), while a stela from Piraeus, also of the fifth century B.C., shows the dog reclining under the banquet couch and gnawing at a hefty hunk of meat (figure 3). The meat in this instance could be explained as a sop. An early Corinthian crater, however, shows leashed dogs underneath the couches of the celebrants which suggests that the details related by Tertullian and Minucius Felix as to the function of the dogs as "the pimps of darkness" in sacral sexual orgies, for all its similarities to a Rube Goldberg mechanism, may have been an ancient artifice (figure 4).

It is of interest to observe that the earliest representation of the dog under the couch, ca. 2500 B.C., is in a scene with two couples copulating in different positions and suggestive at least of the sort of group activity of which the later Christians were accused. Scenes of group sex involving three or more participants are not uncommon in the glyptic art of ancient Mesopotamia. The dog continued on funeral reliefs down to late antiquity, as on the urn of Iulia Eleutheris in the Thermen Museum in Rome showing mourners engaged in *conclamtio mortis* while beneath the bier reposes the persistent canine.

The dog played an important role in the funerary cults at Palmyra and Hatra. At Hatra there appears to have been a sanctuary dedicated to the infernal deity Nergol as a dog (*nrgwl klb'*).

The term *mrzḥ* applied in the Ugaritic text to the place where El imbibed to the point of delirium, diarrhea, and enuresis, and finally to a state resembling death, is of particular interest and importance for the understanding of the nature and purpose of the bacchanalian banquet. This word occurs twice in the Old Testament, Amos 6:7 and Jeremiah 16:5, and the RSV renderings "revelry" in the first instance and "mourning" in the second, reflect the long-standing puzzlement as to the precise meaning of the term. In Amos 6:4–7 the dissolute luxury of the proceedings is explicit:

> They lie on ivory beds,
> Sprawled on their couches,

Figure 3. Funerary relief from Piraeus

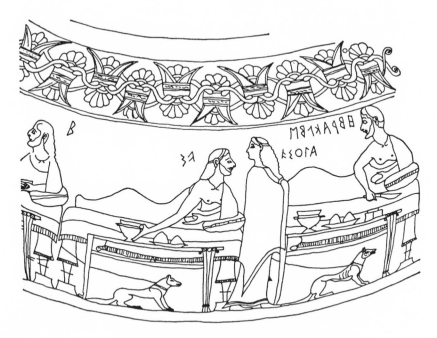

Figure 4. Corinthian crater (mixing bowl) showing leashed dogs under banquet couches

> Eating rams from the flock,
> Bullocks from the stall.
> They chant to the tune of the lyre,
> Like David they improvise song.
> They drink wine from bowls,
> Choicest oils they smear,
> But are not sickened at Joseph's ruin.
> Therefore they will go at the head of the exiles,
> And the sprawlers' banquet cease.

The "sprawlers' banquet," *marzēaḥ sěrûḥîm,* is ambiguous. The root *srḥ* I is applied to an overhanging curtain in Exodus 26:12 and to a spreading vine in Ezekiel 17:6, and possibly to a flowing headdress in Ezekiel 23:15. There is also a root *srḥ* II apparently meaning "be putrid," or the like, in Jeremiah 49:7 and Sirach 42:11.

The couch (*mēsib*) of the king whereon he enjoys, among other things, the fragrance of his lady's perfume, 1:12, in its feminine form *měsibbah* is the postbiblical Hebrew equivalent of the Greek term *symposion,* in which the revelers sprawl on couches.

The expression "*marzēaḥ*-house," *bêṯ marzēaḥ,* is used in Jeremiah 16:5:

> Thus says YHWH:
> Do not enter the *marzēaḥ*-house,
> Do not go to mourn,
> Do not lament for them.
> For I have removed my peace from this people.

[The Septuagint] LXX here rendered *bêṯ marzēaḥ* as *thiasos,* a term which designates a company assembled to celebrate a festival in honor of a deity, or a mourning feast. Jeremiah goes on (Jer. 16:6–9) to describe the funeral celebration which will not take place:

> Great and small will die in this land
> And they will not be buried.
> None shall mourn or lament;
> None shall gash himself,
> None be made bald for them.
> None shall provide a mourning meal
> To comfort him for the dead,
> Nor make him drink the cup of consolation
> For his father and his mother.

You shall not enter the drinking-house
To sit with them,
To eat and to drink.
For thus says YHWH of Hosts,
The God of Israel:
Behold, I am banishing from this place
Before your eyes, and in your days,
The sound of exultation,
The sound of joy,
The sound of the groom,
And the sound of the bride.

The terms "*marzēaḥ*-house," *bêt marzēaḥ,* and "drinking-house," *bet miš-teh,* appear to be roughly synonymous in the passage just cited, as designations of a place in which banquets were held in both mourning and revelry for the dead, with drunkenness and sacral sexual intercourse. The mention of ivory beds, feasting, music and song, wine bibbing, and perfume oil in Amos 6:4–7 and of mourning and lamentation, eating and drinking, the sounds of exultation and joy, and the sounds of groom and bride in Jeremiah 16:6–9 are all features of the funeral feast in the *marzēaḥ*(-house), or the drinking-house.

The drowning of sorrow in the cup of consolation is a practice older than the Irish wake. The rabbis felt it necessary to reform the custom and control the tendency to alcoholic excess at funeral feasts. Ten cups were permitted to be drunk in the house of mourning, but then four extra cups were added as special toasts to various notables, civic and religious leaders, and one in honor of Rabban Gamaliel, so that some became intoxicated and the limit of ten cups was restored. At the festival of Purim, however, it was permissible to drink until one could not tell the difference between Haman and Mordecai. The example of the father of the gods of Ugarit, reeling in drunken delirium, wallowing in excrement and urine, and collapsing as if dead, was on occasion emulated by the Israelites, to judge from the prophet's animadversion, Isaiah 28:7–8:

These, too, reel with wine,
With drink they stagger;
Priest and prophet stagger with drink,
Dazed with wine,
Reeling with drink.
They stagger in ——,
Totter in ———;

> All the tables full of vomit,
> Excrement without place.

The mention of tables full of vomit and excrement in the last couplet suggests that similar terms may have originally stood in lines f and g where MT [Masoretic Text] has the bizarre readings *br'h*, vocalized as *bārô'eh* ("in the seer"), and *pĕlîliyyāh*, "judicial decision," as the setting of their staggering. With very slight change of *br'h* one may restore *bḥr'* ("in excrement"). The word *here'* was considered obscene and the less offensive term *ṣo'āh* ("excretion"), was imposed in Isaiah 36:23 = 2 Kings 18:27. It is harder to guess what term may have been changed to *pĕlîliyyāh*, but the context suggests the common connection and parallel of solid and liquid excreta, as in Isaiah 36:12 and Ugaritic *ḥr'* and *ṯnt*, ("excrement" and "urine"). Isaiah's allusion to priests and prophets reeling among tables strewn with vomit and excrement, and the appalling picture of the drunken father of the gods wallowing in his own filth recall the rabbinic derision of the coprophilia ascribed to the cult of Baal Peor whose worship was alleged to include ceremonial defecation. A Jew was forbidden to relieve himself before the idol, even with the intention of degrading it, since this was the alleged mode of worshiping Baal Peor. A story is told of a certain Jew who entered the shrine of Baal Peor, defecated and wiped himself on the idol's nose and the acolytes praised his devotion saying, "No man ever served this idol thus." It is difficult to know whether this story is based on direct knowledge of such worship or was suggested by one of the meanings of the verb *p'r* in Jewish Aramaic.

While the coprological aspects of the cult of Baal Peor were not especially attractive, there were other features which had potent appeal and to which the Israelites succumbed at the first encounter with the Moabites at Shittim, Numbers 25:1–2, 6–8, and frequently thereafter. The "sacrifices" to which the Moabite women invited their Israelite cousins featured a contact sport which made it possible for Phinehas to skewer an Israelite man and a Moabite woman with a single thrust of the spear, Numbers 25:7–8. Now these festivities are explicitly identified as funeral feasts in Psalms 106:28:

> They yoked themselves to Baal Peor,
> And ate the sacrifices of the dead.

These sacrifices of the dead characterized by sacral sexual intercourse are identified by the rabbis as *marzĕḥîm* in the Sifre (Numbers 131), the same term applied to the setting of El's potation and self-pollution. Midrashic comment further related the marzēaḥ to the Mayumas festival, a celebration which featured wife-swapping. Mayumas festivals were observed along the Mediterranean, especially in port cities like Alexandria, Gaza, Ashkelon and Antioch, with such licentiousness that the Roman rulers felt constrained to ban them. Rabbi Hanan apparently alluded to such rites in his comment that "it was done in the cities of the Sea what was not done in the generation of the Flood." The equation of Marzēaḥ and Mayumas is also made in the mosaic map of the sixth-century church at Madeba which labels the Transjordanian area in which the Baal-Peor apostasy occurred as "*Betomarseas* (i.e., Beth Marzēaḥ) alias (*ho kai*) Maioumas." Several scholars have recently treated the term *marzēaḥ* in detail, and only a brief summary with a few supplementary observations need be given for the present concern to understand the nature of the marzēaḥ and suggest a relationship to the Song of Songs.

Considerable information on the marzēaḥ comes to us from Palmyra in the form of dedicatory inscriptions and tessarae decorated with banquet scenes and bearing inscriptions mentioning the term *mrzḥ*. J. T. Milik has brought together the Semitic and Greek epigraphic materials dealing with these celebrations by gods and mortals with chapters on the vocabulary of the Palmyrene tessarae and inscriptions, and other data on the religious associations at Palmyra, Dura, Hatra, Syria, Phoenicia, and among the Nabateans. This work is a veritable treasure-trove of information on the funeral feasts, with data which may be correlated with the Ugaritic materials to provide new and provocative insights which may have relevance for the understanding of the Song of Songs. Some data from Milik's study will be briefly noticed in supplements to the commentary which had been completed before Milik's work appeared. There is much in Milik's study which will stimulate further research and discussion.

The members of the association were termed in Aramaic *bny mrzḥ'*, "children of the *mrzḥ*," and specific deities were sometimes designated, e.g., *bny mrzḥ nbw*, "members of the mrzḥ of Nabu." The most popular association at Palmyra was apparently associated with Bel (Baal), to judge from the numerous tessarae which mention the priests of Bel. Each *mrzḥ* had a chief, Phoenician *rb mrzḥ*, Aramaic *rb mrzḥ'*, Greek *symposiarchēs*. The priests of Bel at Palmyra were organized in a college headed by the chief priest, *archiereus kai symposiarchēs*, who served also as eponym for dating the acts of the association. The symposiarch of the priests of Bel was also chief of all other symposia of the city and had charge of the "house of distribution, *bt qsm'*. An inscription erected in recognition of the services of a certain Yarḥai Agrippa in the year A.D. 243 notes that in his leadership of the symposia he "served the gods and presided over the distribution (*qsm'*) a whole year and supplied old wine for the priests a whole year from his house."

The Akkadian documents from Ugarit which mention the marzēaḥ suggest that it was an important institution. The king Niqmepa bequeathed "a house of the marzēaḥ-men" to the marzēaḥ-men and their children. A house of the marzēaḥ-men of (the god) Šatran was taken over for official use, but another house was given in its place. A vineyard of Ishtar was divided between the marzēaḥ-men of the city of Ari and those of the city of Siyanni. In a fragmentary Ugaritic alphabetic text (2032) there are five or six occurrences of the phrase *mrzḥ'n[. . .]* and in line 2 occur the words *šd kr[. . .]*, "field vineya[rd]." Eissfeldt proposed the restoration *mrzḥ 'n[t]* and suggested that the text may deal with the bequest of several vineyards to the marzēaḥ (Kultverein) of Anat.

The connection between the marzēaḥ and the funeral feast, attested in both biblical and rabbinic references, is confirmed by Ugarit data. Although there are no explicit references to the funeral character of the sacrificial banquet in which all the gods become drunk but El sits in his *mrzḥ* and topes till he sinks down as if dead, and although there are no hints of sexual activities in connection with this occasion which centers on El's hangover and its medicinal relief, there are elsewhere hints of sexual activity in connection with funeral feasts at Ugarit. The so-called Rephaim Texts, thus designated because of the frequent occurrence of the term (*rpum* in the nominative case and *rpim* in the oblique cases), which in biblical usage is connected with the departed dead, denizens of the netherworld (cf. Isa. 14:9, 26:14, 19; Ps. 88:11; Prov. 2:18, 9:18, 21:16; Job 26:5), supply all the elements of a marzēaḥ, a funeral feast to which the gods and the deified dead are invited to join with the mourners in a seven-day celebration with flesh and wine and with hints, at least, of sexual activity. The Rephaim Texts apparently belong to the Aqht Epic and fit into the action following the murder of Danel's son Aqht. In spite of the fragmentary state of the texts and numerous lexical and grammatical uncertainties, it is apparent that Danel invites the Rephaim to a *mrz'* (122:1), a variant form of *mrzḥ*, in a shrine (*atr*, "place") in his house.

From the various strands of evidence, we gather that the marzēaḥ was a religious institution which included families and owned houses for meetings and vineyards for supply of wine, that the groups met periodically to celebrate seven-day feasts with rich food and drink and sometimes with sexual orgies. The biblical and rabbinic identification of these revels as funeral feasts is illustrated by a wealth of sepulchural sculpture depicting the deceased as participating in the banquet. The charge that the early Christians in their initiation rites immolated infants and ate their flesh and drank their blood is of interest in light of the cannibalistic language of the Eucharist in which the bread and wine are Christ's flesh and blood. The eating of the flesh and drinking of the juices of deceased loved ones is a primitive practice and is attested also at Ugarit. In a brief vignette inscribed on the back of a lexical text, the goddess Anat is depicted as consuming the flesh and blood of her brother consort (Baal):

> Anat went and waxed mad (?)
> At the beauty of her brother,
> And at the handsomeness of her brother,
> For he was fair.
> She ate his flesh without a knife,
> She drank his blood without a cup.

While we are not informed whether Anat's beauteous brother was alive or dead when she thus consumed him, we may reasonably assume that he was defunct and that this was a mourning rite motivated by what anthropologists have termed "morbid affection." M. Astour related Anat's cannibalism to the raw flesh feasts of the Dionysiac and Orphic orgies. It is apparent that the Christian Eucharist and Love-Feast, as well as the Jewish qiddush, represent radical reformations of the ancient funeral feasts with elimination of such gross features as cannibalism, drunkenness, and sexual license. Paul's rebuke of unseemly behavior at the sacred meals (1 Cor. 11:21, Rom. 13:13) and the charges ridiculed by Tertullian and Minucius Felix suggest that there were those who resisted reform and persisted in the old ways and this is confirmed by the repeated condemnations of other Fathers of the church.

In his first letter to the Christians at Corinth the apostle Paul was distressed about licentious conduct in the festal meals when they partook of "spiritual" (pneumatic) food and drink, 1 Corinthians 10–11. Paul cited in censure of the Christian misbehavior the example of the Israelites' mode of worship of the Golden Calf: "The people sat down to eat and drink and rose up to sport (*paizein*)," 1 Corinthians 10:7. The kind of sport implied by the Hebrew term in Exodus 32:6 (*lĕṣaḥēq*) is clear from Isaac's uxorious play in Genesis 26:8. Paul explicitly inveighed against fornication in these pneumatic feasts and cited as a warning the fate of the twenty-three thousand (give or take a thousand; cf. Num. 25:9) who fell in a single day, with obvious reference to the affair at the shrine at Baal Peor, Numbers 25. We are told in Psalm 106:28 that the cult of Baal Peor involved the eating of sacrifices for the dead. The rabbis further identify the festivities of Baal Peor as *marzĕḥîm* and relate them to the infamous Mayumas festivals, a correlation supported by the Madeba Map which labels the area in which the scandal occurred as Marzēah-House, alias Mayumas.

The etymology of the term *marzēaḥ* remains unclear. Joseph Qimḥi, followed by his son David, connected the word with Arabic *mirziḥ* alleged to signify a vehement voice or loud cry as in mourning or revelry. Eissfeldt posited a meaning "unite" for the root *rzḥ* and took the word to designate a cultic union, "Kultverein." B. Porten regarded Eissfeldt's distinction between two supposed homonyms *rzḥ*, "shout," and *rzḥ*, "unite," to be arbitrary. The basic meaning of *rzḥ* in Arabic is to fall down from fatigue or other weakness and remain prostrate without power to rise; it may be used of a man, a camel, or a grapevine. A *marzaḥ* is a place where a camel collapses from fatigue and a *mirzaḥ* is a prop for a fallen grapevine. The collapse of El in his *mrzḥ* and the *mirzāḥ* of sprawled ones Amos 6:7 comport with this sense of the term. The celebrants at a *marziḥ, thiasos,* or symposium recline on couches and after several rounds of drink would, no doubt, be aptly described as sprawling, or perhaps even more relaxed to the state of comatose stupor.

Whatever the etymology, it is apparent that the **marziḥ* designated a bacchanalian celebration roughly synonymous with the Greek *thiasos* and *symposion*. The "Marzēah House" is thus virtually synonymous with the "Banquet House," *bêt mišteh* literally "house of drinking." Rabbi Akiba anathematized those who trilled verses of the Song of Songs in "drinking houses" and this has been understood to mean that the good rabbi objected to the singing of snatches of the most holy song in the wine shops or taverns. The banquet house, or drinking house, however, was not a tavern or pub, but rather a place for sacral feasting and drinking, as evidenced by Belshazzar's feast in the *bêt mištěyā'*, Daniel 5:10, with the appropriation of the holy vessels taken from the Jerusalem Temple for sacral drinking in praise of the heathen gods by the king and his nobles and courtesans, Daniel 5:1–4, 10. The more explicit term "house of the drinking of wine," *bêt mišteh hayyayin,* is used in Esther 7:8 when the king returned to the wine fest and found Haman prostrate on the couch with Esther, Haman apparently being in a drunken stupor and unaware of his predicament. In the festival of Purim which is supposed to celebrate and commemorate the deliverance of the Jews through the elimination of their enemy Haman by the counterplot of Mordecai and Esther, it is nevertheless permissible and even obligatory to become more than moderately inebriated. It has been suggested that Purim is in reality a disguised "feast of the dead," related to the Persian All Souls' Day, *Farvardigan,* and that the feasting and giftgiving are survivals of offerings to the dead. The avoidance of the name of the God of Israel in the book of Esther was explained as due to this original connection with the cult of the dead. It is of interest in this connection that Esther and the Canticle are the only biblical books which make no mention of the ineffable name.

The unique term "house of wine" in Song of Songs 2:4 is manifestly an elliptical expression for "house of the drinking of wine," as in Esther 7:8, since a musty wine cellar would hardly be an appropriate setting for the activity envisaged:

> He brought me into the wine house,
> His intent toward me Love.

Other details of the Canticle also are suggestive of orgiastic revelry. The lady requests stimulants to renew her jaded desire, 2:5,

> Sustain me with raisin cakes,
> Brace me with apples,
> For faint from love am I.

These raisin cakes (cf. Hos. 3:1) survive today in Purim pastries called Hamantaschen (corrupted from German *Mohntaschen,* "poppy pockets," from the practice of stuffing them with poppy seeds). These cuneiform tarts have nothing to do with Haman's three-cornered hat or his ears, but probably originally represented the pubes of Queen Esther = Ishtar, Queen of Heaven. The mandrakes mentioned in 7:14 give further hint of interest in stimulation. The repeated adjuration, 2:7, 3:5, 8:4, relating to the arousal of love when it is willing, suggests protracted and repeated amative activity. The reference in 7:10 to the fine wine gliding over the lips of sleepers (if one follows MT against the versions) is understandable on the supposition that one could continue to imbibe even in sleep, or while unconscious, by means of a drinking tube or with an attendant to dribble the wine through the lips. In competitive drinking, contestants may recline and drink through tubes for maximum intake and effect. The dead too were provided with drink through tubes leading into the tombs. Thus the "sleepers" over whose lips the wine drips may refer to the funerary libation. It is striking, and perhaps no accident, that this verse evoked for the rabbis the image of deceased scholars whose lips move in the grave whenever a saying is cited in their name.

The references to myrrh, spice, honey, wine, and milk in a single verse of the Canticle, 5:1, are suggestive of the funeral feast since all these elements are associated with funerary rites and sacrifices. Myrrh and spices were used in anointing the corpse for burial (cf. Mark 16:1; Luke 24:1; John 19:39–40). Spices were also used as condiments in the savory stew for the funeral meal. Ezekiel 24:10 mentions the mixing of spices in the preparation of the pottage symbolic of Babylon's evil:

> Heap the wood,
> Kindle the fire,
> Prepare the meat,
> Mix the spices,
> Let the bones cook.

(The emendation of *weharqah hammerqāḥāh,* "mix the spices," on the basis of LXX *kai elattōthē ho zōmos,* "and let the liquor be boiled away," is a dubious procedure.) Libations for the dead in Homeric times included honey, wine, and milk, as when Ulysses poured to the congregation of the dead libations of honey and milk and sweet wine (*Odyssey* 11.28ff.) and Achilles laid beside Patroclus's bier jars of honey and oil (*Iliad* 23.172). In all parts of the Aryan world honey was a food sacred to the dead. In India the *pitaras* ("fathers"), were supplied rice soup mixed with honey, similar to the mead of barley water and honey served by the peasants of White Russia to their ancestors. In Greece honey cakes (*melitoutta*) were given to the dead and were believed also to appease the infernal watchdog Cerberus. Honey cakes continue as an essential part of the commemorative funeral meal among Lithuanian and Russian peasants. Herodotus reported that the Babylonians buried their dead in honey. The Spartans reportedly brought home the body of King Agesipolis preserved in honey and that of King Agesilaus in wax. A first-century epitaph from Crete bids the parents of three defunct brothers bring offerings of honeycomb and incense.

The open invitation of [Song of Songs] 5:1ef,

> Eat, friends, drink,
> Be drunk with love!

suggests the sort of climax to be expected in a thoroughly inebriated mixed group. Similar invitations are given in the Ugaritic texts, as when El says to his erstwhile spouse Asherah:

> Eat, yea drink!
> Eat from the tables meat,
> Drink from the jars wine;
> From a gold cup the blood of the vine.
> Lo, the affection of King El will arouse you,
> The Bull's love will excite you.

Or the invitation to the votaries in the ritual portion of the "Birth of the Beautiful Gods"

> Eat of the food, Ay!
> Drink of the foaming wine, Ay!
> Peace, O King,
> Peace, O Queen,
> O entrants and archers.

These invitations recall the frescoes of the catacombs and some of the uninhibited scenes which create the impression of a cosy drinking party, as described by F. van der Meer:

Above the heads of the serving girls, who are hastening to supply the guests, stand the words: "Agape, mix my wine! Eirene, give me some warm water!"—phrases which certainly do not elevate the ladies Love and Peace to the status of heavenly allegories; incidentally these ladies make their appearance no less than four times—the painter was obviously repeating a stereotype.

Among the slogans in these scenes of Christian love feasts for the dead were the cry *Refrigera bene* which van der Meer rendered "Take good refreshment, eat and drink!" and *eis agapēn* ("To the heavenly feast," literally "to love") and above all *In pace*. According to van der Meer:

The people who chiselled these mystical allusions did their work in the midst of pagans and in the midst of persecution; but that reverent atmosphere is now definitely a thing of the past. The food upon the tables, once a thing so full of meaning, has achieved vestigial survival, but those at the table now have manners more suited to a pothouse, while the crude decorations represent nothing more than the husks of an ancient symbolism which now garnish the wine jugs of an ordinary, and distinctly convivial, wake!

Sepulchural gardens were common in the Graeco-Roman world, adjacent to the tombs, hence the technical term "garden tomb," *kēpotafion, cepotafium*. Strabo described the district west of Alexandria as containing many gardens (*kēpoi*) and tombs (*tafai*). Jocelyn M. C. Toynbee cites several inscriptions and documents referring to funerary gardens. Of particular interest is an inscription found near Rome, dating probably to the second century, set up by the parents in memory of their ten-year-old son. The text includes a prayer to Osiris to give the dead lad cool water. The parents made for the boy "an eternal bridal chamber" (*aiōnion nymphōna*) and for themselves in expectation of their death a garden tomb (*kēpotafion*). Toynbee wondered whether the "eternal bridal chamber" was "for mystic marriage with the god." Extensive evidence associating sacral sexual rites with mortuary celebrations should relieve somewhat the puzzlement at the designation of a tomb as an "eternal bridal chamber." Toynbee goes on to cite some of the very interesting Latinized versions of Greek funerary terminology. In addition to *cepotafium* and the diminutive *cepotafiolum*, there are the Latin terms *hortus, horti*, and *hortulus*. These sepulchural plots are frequently described as surrounded by an enclosure wall (*murus, maceria*). The enclosed garden is reminiscent of the *gan/l nā'ûl*, the *hortus conclusus*, of Canticles 4:12.

In addition to the general words for buildings used in the funerary inscriptions in association with the gardens, such as edifice (*aedificia*) and monument (*monumenta*), there are words that refer specifically to the places where the funerary feasts were celebrated. There are references to dining rooms (*cenacula*), eating houses (*tabernae*), summer houses (*tricliae*), bars or lounges (*diaetae*), sun terraces (*solaria*), storehouses (*horrea*), and even, in one case, apparently, rooms to let(?) or brothels(?) (*stabula* and *meritoria*). In the sepulchural gardens were paths (*itinera*). Water was supplied by cisterns (*cisternae*), basins (*piscinae*), channels (*canales*), wells (*putei*), and pools (*lacus*). The funerary garden is variously described as a small estate (*praedolium*), a field (*ager*), or as orchards (*pomaria* or *pomariola*). One tomb was adorned with vines, fruit trees, flowers, and plants of all kinds, another with trees, vines and roses, and yet another with a vineyard and enclosure walls. The funerary terminology is strikingly similar to certain expressions of the Canticle.

The garden-tomb setting and terminology of the Graeco-Roman mortuary cult recalls the reprimand of Second (or Third?) Isaiah, Isa. 65:1–7, depicting Israel's God as constantly waiting and making overtures to an unresponsive people addicted to abominable rites in the funerary gardens:

I was available to those who did not ask,
Accessible to those who did not seek.
I said, "Here I am! Here I am!"
To a nation that did not call on my name.
I spread my hands all day
To a rebellious people
Who walk in a no-good way,
Following their own devices,
A people who provoke me
To my face, constantly,
Sacrificing in the gardens,
Burning incense on bricks,
Sitting in the tombs,
Spending the night in crypts,
Eating pig meat,
Carrion broth in their vessels.
They say, "Stand back;
Don't touch me, I'm holy to you."
These are smoke in my nose,
A fire that burns all day.
Lo, it is written before me:
"I will not be quiet, I will requite
I will requite in the bosom
Your crimes and your fathers' crimes
Together," says the Lord.
"Because they burned incense on the mountains,
Disgraced me on the hills,
I will measure out their wage
Promptly on their lap."

The Qumran Isaiah Scroll offers in 65:3d a reading radically different from MT. In place of MT's "and burning incense on the bricks," the Qumran text presents the provocative reading *wynqw ydym 'l h'bnym* ("and they suck / cleanse hands upon / as well as the stones"). In view of the well-attested euphemistic use of "hand" for phallus (cf. 5:4a) and the possibility that *'l h'bnym* in Exodus 1:16 refers to genitalia in general or testicles in particular, the verb *ynqw* could be connected either with *ynq* ("suck"), or *nqy*, meaning "cleanse" in the factitive or D stem. Fellatio would inevitably be suggested by *ynq*. It is hard to imagine how cleansing hands could be bad.

An Old Babylonian text published by J. J. Finkelstein has a bearing on the present concern with mortuary meals. Finkelstein's masterly treatment of the document established its *Sitz im Leben,* that is, the reason it was written and the manner in which it was used. The text lists the ancestors of Ammiṣaduqa, last king of the First Dynasty of Babylon, and includes collectively "the dynasties of the Amorites, the Haneans, the Gutium, the dynasty not recorded on this tablet, and the soldier(s) who fell while on *perilous campaigns* for their (his) lord, princes, princesses, all persons from East to West who have neither caretaker (*pāqidum*) nor attendant (*sāhirum*). All these are invited:

> Come ye, e(a)t this, (drin)k this, (and)
> Ammiṣaduqa, son of Ammiditana, the king of Babylon, bless ye.

The restorations of the imperatives *aklā* ("eat ye") and *šityā* ("drink ye") in lines 39–40 are suggested by the traces of the poorly preserved signs as well as by the unmistakable context of the whole as a *kispu* offering which consisted of food and drink for the dead.

> The nature and function of the text as a whole is hardly open to doubt: it is the invocation to an actual memorial service to the dead, the central action of which was the offering to the *etemmū*—ghosts or spirits of the dead—of the *kispu,* which consisted of food and drink.

It is no ordinary *kispu* ceremony, however, of the standard sort held semimonthly on the first and sixteenth day.

> The inclusion of the spirits of other than the dead ancestors, including even the ghosts of anyone and everyone "from East to West" who otherwise has none to offer them the *kispum,* suggests that the occasion was an extraordinary one, but the text itself offers no clue as to what it might have been. The performance might still have been scheduled for the first or sixteenth day of the month, but this would have been coincidental with some other momentous occasion which called for a more inclusive mortuary "feast." One might think of the coronation of the new king as an occasion suitable for such an expression of royal "largesse"—when perhaps even the living population received something above their normally miserable fare. What could be more appropriate for Ammiṣaduqa, as the newly crowned *šar mīšarim,* than to demonstrate his concern

for his people's welfare by a special food distribution to all—
to the dead as well as the living?

The present writer ventures to suggest that the occasion in question
was a sort of Hallowmas, a feast for All Saints and Souls.

The affirmation 8:6c,d "For Love is strong as Death, / Passion fierce
as Hell" has been generally recognized as the theme and message of the
Song of Songs. This is also the assurance of Paul's praise of love in
1 Corinthians 13:8: "Love never quits" (*hē agapē oudepote ekpiptei*).
"There are three things that last, Faith, Hope, Love—and Love is the
greatest." The nature of the Love (*hē agapē*) which Paul commended to
the Corinthians had little in common with the sort of love feasts which
they were wont to celebrate. Nevertheless, these pagan love feasts were
also a response to death with the assertion of life in its most basic modes
of expression, eating, drinking, and copulation, all requisite for the continuation of life. Mother Earth, from whom man comes and to whom
he returns, she who creates, nourishes, destroys, and takes man back into
her ample womb, was worshiped at the ancestral graves with love feasts
and commemorative rites to ensure the continuation of life. It is no accident that tombstones and memorial stelae are sometimes distinctly phallic in form, as often with the Greek *herma,* and that the term *yād* ("hand")
in Ugaritic and Hebrew is applied to the phallus and in Hebrew to a
memorial stela (1 Sam. 15:12; 2 Sam. 18:18; Isa. 56:5), while the terms
for "memory" and "phallus" appear to be related to the same root, *＊ḏkr,*
zkr.

The epistle of Jude inveighs against impious persons who had
sneaked into the Christian community and had perverted the grace of
God to an excuse for fornication and unnatural lust. These people are
described, Jude 12, as "reefs (*spilades*) in your love feasts (*en tais agapais
humōn*)." In a parallel passage, 2 Peter 2:13, they are called "blots (*spiloi*)
and blemishes (*mōmoi*) who revel in their love feasts" (choosing the variant *agapais* over *apatais,* "dissipations"). The charges and invectives laid
on these subversives, Jude 8–16, 2 Peter 2:4–22, stress sexual licentiousness. The point of interest here is the explicit connection of this sort of
conduct with the love feasts. Passing over the question of the relation of
the Agape and the Eucharist, it will suffice to stress the original and
essential character of these celebrations as mortuary meals, continuing
the ancient and well-nigh universal practice of providing refreshment for
the dead and sharing it with them in a communal and commemorative
meal. Such celebrations from time immemorial had not infrequently fea-

tured orgiastic revelry, drunkenness, gluttony, cannibalism, incest, and sundry other excesses. In the early church the cult of the martyrs evolved quite naturally from the need to offer a tolerable substitute for these irrepressible practices. As long as the offerings, whether to ancestors or martyrs, remained moderately decent affairs, there was no need to prohibit them. The charge that Christians offered food and wine to appease the shades of the martyrs Augustine rebutted with the argument that the altars were built to God in honor of the martyrs and not to the martyrs as if they were gods; honor was paid to the martyrs merely to encourage others to emulate them and share in their merits. It was doubtless difficult for newcomers to Christianity to appreciate the subtle difference between outwardly similar procedures in offerings to the ancestors and the martyrs. The toleration of the memorials for the martyrs was probably a concession to recent converts who were reluctant to relinquish the pleasures of the old-time revels. The trouble came when the grosser features of the pagan celebrations were carried over into the Christian love feasts, as the protests of early Christian writers attest. Augustine was tolerant toward the harmless sort of devotion to the saints and martyrs which his mother practiced, but not toward the drunken carousals carried on in some circles. When his mother Monica first came to Milan, she went to church with a basket of food and wine for the graves of the saints, as she had been accustomed to do in Africa, but was informed by the porter that this practice had been banned by the bishop. Augustine well understood the reasons for this ban imposed by Ambrose, since these meals for the saints were too much like pagan *parentalia* and served as an excuse for drunkenness. There were those who worshiped at the tombs, set food before the dead, drank to excess, and then attributed gluttony and drunkenness to religion. One should not judge Christianity, Augustine argued, by the behavior of the masses, who remained superstitious or were so enslaved to sensual pleasures that they forgot their promises to God. In his sermons Augustine tried to persuade the people that such excesses were pagan and did not derive from the stock and vine of justice of our patriarchs. Sirach 30:18, which compares the placing of food on graves to putting dainties before a mouth that is closed, was explained as referring to a sick person who refuses food, since the Patriarchs kept no *parentalia*. Tobit 4:7, however, commands the deposit of food and pouring of wine on the graves of the just, but not on those of the wicked, and from this Augustine deduced that the faithful may perform this sort of *memorial* for their relatives provided it is done with pious intention. Those who persisted in heathen revelry, however, were blasted by Augustine: "The martyrs hate your wine jugs and cooking pots and your gluttony."

> There they bring bread and wine to the grave and call the dead by name. How often after his death they must have called out the name of the wealthy glutton when they got drunk in his mausoleum, and yet not a drop fell on his parched tongue.
>
> *(Enarrationes in Psalmos)*

Similarly Zeno of Verona inveighed in the style of the prophet Amos:

> God is displeased by those who run along to the gravesides, offer their lunch to stinking corpses and then in their desire to eat and drink suddenly, with pot and glass, conjure up martyrs at the most unfitting places.

The Donatists, in particular, were charged with utter wantonness, as

> those gangs of vagabonds who bury their own selves upon their graves in loathesome promiscuity, seducing one another into all manner of vice.

Madden in her summation modestly concluded that

> out of the pagan customs in honor of the dead, abuses developed in the festivals held to honor the memory of the martyrs. It became necessary to take measures against these abuses. The allusions to the traces of these customs relating to the honoring of the dead show that this phase of paganism had a strong hold on the hearts of the people, even after they had become Christians.

It is beyond the scope of this present effort to attempt any systematic treatment of funeral cults in the ancient world. The preceding discussion was intended merely to suggest that certain features of the Song of Songs may be understood in the light of the considerable and growing evidences that funeral feasts in the ancient Near East were love feasts celebrated with wine, women, and song. The Greek term *agapē*, LOVE, attached to these feasts certainly included *eros* as well as *philia*, to judge from the condemnations of drunkenness, fornication, and other excesses in the New Testament and the Church Fathers. The appearance of some of the characteristic terms of the Canticle in the Ugaritic mythological and ritual texts, especially in connection with the term *marziḥ, and in the inscriptions from Palmyra which confirm and elucidate the connection of the *marziḥ/thiasos/symposion* with the funeral feast, opens new possibilities, yet to be fully tested and exploited, for the understanding of the cultic origins of the Canticles. This approach seems capable of explaining the Canticles better than any other and is able to subsume aspects of other modes of interpretation as enfolding elements of truth. The connection of the Canticle with the funeral feast as expressive of the deepest and most constant human concern for Life and Love in the ever-present face of Death adds new insight and appreciation of our pagan predecessors who responded to Death with affirmations and even gross demonstrations of the power and persistence of Life and Love:

> *Kî 'azzāh kammawet 'ahăbāh*
>
> *Hoti krataia hōs thanatos agapē*
>
> *Quia fortis est ut mors dilectio*

For Love is strong as Death.

Love's Lyrics Redeemed

Phyllis Trible

Love is bone of bone and flesh of flesh. Thus I hear the Song of Songs. It speaks from lover to lover with whispers of intimacy, shouts of ecstasy, and silences of consummation. At the same time, its unnamed voices reach out to include the world in their symphony of eroticism. This movement between the private and the public invites all companions to enter a garden of delight.

Genesis 2–3 is the hermeneutical key with which I unlock this garden. That narrative began with the development of Eros in four episodes: the forming of the earth creature, the planting of a garden, the making of animals, and the creation of sexuality. Alas, however, the fulfillment proclaimed when 'îš and 'iššâ became one flesh disintegrated through disobedience. As a result, Yahweh God drove out generic man and invisible woman from the garden, and "at the east of the garden of Eden he placed the cherubim, and a flaming sword which turned every way, to guard the way to the tree of life" (Gen. 3:24, RSV [Revised Standard Version]). Clearly, Genesis 2–3 offers no return to the garden of creation. And yet, as Scripture interpreting Scripture, it provides my clue for entering another garden of Eros, the Song of Songs. Through expansions, omissions, and reversals, this poetry recovers the love that is bone of bone and flesh of flesh. In other words, the Song of Songs redeems a love story gone awry. Taking clues from Genesis 2, then, let us acquire first an overview of the form and content of the Song.

From *God and the Rhetoric of Sexuality.* © 1978 by Fortress Press.

READING THE MUSICAL SCORE

Expanding upon the lyrics of eroticism in Genesis 2, three human voices compose this new song. They belong to a woman, a man, and a group of women, the daughters of Jerusalem. Independent of logical progression or plot development, these voices flow freely and spontaneously to yield a series of metaphors in which many meanings intertwine simultaneously. At times, the standard, the figurative, and the euphemistic converge so compellingly that one cannot discern where vehicle ends and tenor begins. Often the language is elusive, holding its treasures in secret for the lovers themselves. Occasionally the identity of the speaker is uncertain, creating a problem for observers but not for participants who know that in Eros all voices mingle. Hence, the poetry of the Song resists calculations and invites imagination. The visual must be heard; the auditory, seen. Love itself blends sight, sound, sense, and non-sense. In these ways, the voices of the Song of Songs extol and enhance the creation of sexuality in Genesis 2.

Of the three speakers, the woman is the most prominent. She opens and closes the entire Song, her voice dominant throughout. By this structural emphasis her equality and mutuality with the man is illuminated. The arrangement recalls the stress placed upon the woman at the conclusion of Genesis 2: although equal with the man in creation, she was, nonetheless, elevated in emphasis by the design of the story. In the Song of Songs, accent upon the female is further increased by the presence of the daughters of Jerusalem. As a foil and complement to the lovers, this group aids the flow of the action. Women, then, are the principal creators of the poetry of eroticism.

Strikingly, God does not speak in the Song; nor is the deity even mentioned. This divine absence parallels the withdrawal of Yahweh God in Genesis 2 precisely where the poem of eroticism emerged. After making the woman and bringing her to the transformed earth creature, the deity disappeared from scene one. Then the earth creature spoke for the first time:

> This, finally, bone of my bones
> and flesh of my flesh.
> This shall be called 'iššâ
> because from 'îš was differentiated this.
>
> (Gen. 2:23)

Just as the tenor of this poem continues in the Song of Songs, so appropriately does its setting. Yahweh God, who created male and female, withdraws when lovers discover themselves, speak the revelation, and become one flesh.

The cyclic design of Genesis 2 is also reflected and developed in the Song. Originally, the creation of humanity found its fulfillment in the creation of sexuality: the earth creature became two, male and female, and those two became one flesh. With such an erotic completion, the Song of Songs begins, continues, and concludes. As a symphony of love, it unfolds in five major movements of varying lengths. At the conclusions of the first four sections, the woman utters a refrain that both separates and joins these movements. It begins, "I adjure you, O daughters of Jerusalem" (RSV). Clusters of verbal motifs that precede this refrain further interrelate the five movements, yielding an ebb and a flow among the images of the Song. An examination of the beginnings and endings of these movements shows the cyclic pattern of the overall composition.

The introductory movement extends from 1:2 to 2:7. By speaking first *about* her lover, rather than directly *to* him, the woman invites us to enter their circle of intimacy:

> O that he would kiss me with the kisses of his mouth!
> (1:2)

With the words of her mouth she reaches many; for the kisses of her mouth she desires only one. And by the end of the movement her yearnings are realized:

> His left hand is under my head,
>   and his right hand embraces me!
> (2:6)

This verse appears again at the conclusion of the fourth movement, thus providing one of the many verbal links between sections. Since, with these words, the woman's desire has been fulfilled, she completes the introductory movement by imploring the daughters of Jerusalem to let love happen according to its own rhythm:

> I adjure you, O daughters of Jerusalem,
>   by the gazelles or the hinds of the field,
> that you stir not up nor awaken love
>   until it please.
> (2:7, RSV)

Having begun the first movement by seeking the touch of her lover's mouth, the woman commences the second (2:8–3:5) by invoking the speech of his lips:

> The voice of my lover!
> Behold, he comes,
> leaping upon the mountains,
> bounding over the hills.
> (2:8, RSV* [Revised
> Standard Version
> with author's
> emendations])

She concludes this section by seeking and finding her man:

> Upon my bed by night
> I sought him whom my *nephesh* [soul] loves;
> I sought him, but found him not;
> I called him, but he gave no answer.
> "I will rise now and go about the city,
> in the streets and in the squares;
> I will seek him whom my *nephesh* loves."
> I sought him but found him not.
> The watchmen found me,
> as they went about in the city.
> Him whom my *nephesh* loves, have you seen?
> Scarcely had I passed them,
> when I found him whom my *nephesh* loves.
> I held him, and would not let him go
> until I had brought him into my mother's house,
> and into the chamber of her that conceived me.
> (3:1–4, RSV*)

The motifs of the search, the watchmen, and the mother's house surface again in various combinations in the conclusions of the third and fourth movements. Coming together here in the encounter of love, they allow the woman to close this second movement exactly as she did the first. Thus, she implores the daughters of Jerusalem to let love happen according to its own rhythm (3:5).

She opens the third movement (3:6–5:8) with a question about her lover:

> What is that coming up from the wilderness,
> like a column of smoke,

perfumed with myrrh and frankincense,
> with all the fragrant powders of the merchant?
>> (3:6, RSV)

To end this section, she returns, with variations, to two of the themes
at the conclusion of the second movement: the seeking, but not the finding, of the lover and her discovery by the watchmen, who this time not
only fail to help but actually assault her:

> My *nephesh* failed because of him.
> I sought him, but found him not;
>> I called him, but he gave no answer.
> The watchmen found me,
>> as they went about in the city;
> they beat me, they wounded me,
> they took away my mantle,
>> those watchmen of the walls.
>>> (5:6c–7, RSV★)

Exact verbal correspondences between the endings of movements two
and three establish parallelism in their structure and content. The differences between them, on the other hand, sustain the tempo and flow of
the poetry. Point and counterpoint shape the rhythm of love:

3:1–3a (Second Movement)	*5:6b–7 (Third Movement)*
Upon my bed by night	My *nephesh* failed because of
I sought him whom my	him.
nephesh loves;	
I sought him but found him not;	I sought him, but found him not;
I called him but he gave no	I called him, but he gave no
answer.	answer.
"I will rise now and go about the	
city,	
in the streets and in the	
squares;	
I will seek him whom my *nephesh*	
loves."	
I sought him but found him not.	
The watchmen found me,	The watchmen found me,
as they went about in the city.	as they went about in the city;
(RSV)	

> they beat me, they wounded me,
>   they took away my mantle,
>   those watchmen of the walls.
>
> (RSV*)

At the very end of the third movement, the woman alters the refrain of adjuration to fit the situation that now exists. Since, contrary to the ending of the second movement (3:4), she does not find her lover, she enlists the daughters of Jerusalem in her search:

> I adjure you, O daughters of Jerusalem,
>   if you find my lover,
> that you tell him
>   I am sick with love.
>
> (5:8, RSV*)

The words "I am sick with love" repeat a line from the closing sentiments of the first section (2:5), thereby showing another interplay among the motifs of the poem. Although these words led to fulfillment in the first movement, here they but long for consummation.

Linked closely to the third movement, the fourth (5:9–8:4) commences with questions by the daughters, who are responding to the woman's plea in the preceding refrain of adjuration:

> What is your lover more than another lover,
>   O fairest among women?
> What is your lover more than another lover
>   that you thus adjure us?
>
> (5:9, RSV*)

This interrogative style parallels the woman's question at the beginning of the third section. And the closing speech (8:1–3) of the fourth movement belongs again to the woman. She caresses the man with her voice:

> O that you were like a brother to me,
>   that nursed at my mother's breast!
> If I met you outside, I would kiss you,
>   and none would despise me.
> I would lead you and bring you
>   into the house of my mother,
>   and into the chamber of her that conceived me.
> I would give you spiced wine to drink,
>   the juice of my pomegranates.

His left hand is under my head,
and his right hand embraces me!
(8:1–3, RSV★)

Like the end of the third section, this conclusion also returns, with variations, to motifs first appearing at the end of the second movement: finding the lover and bringing him to the house of the mother who conceived her. In the second movement, the woman sought the help of the watchmen and then spoke about her actions toward her lover (3:1–3). Now in the fourth, she addresses her intentions to him directly. Though her reference to "none would despise me" may allude to the watchmen who have since assaulted her, that group is not involved in this ending. Once again, however, exact verbal correspondences between the conclusions of two movements confirm the parallelism in their structure and content, while, on the other hand, differences between them enhance the rhythm of the poetry:

3:3b–4 (Second Movement)	*8:1–2a (Fourth Movement)*
Him whom my *nephesh* loves, have you seen?	O that you were like a brother to me, that nursed at my mother's breast!
Scarcely had I passed them when I found him whom my *nephesh* loves.	If I found you outside, I would kiss you, and none would despise me.
I held him and would not let him go until I had brought him into my mother's house, and into the chamber of her that conceived me.	I would lead you and bring you into my mother's house and into the chamber of her that conceived me.
(RSV★)	(RSV★)

The word *kiss* in the speech of the woman to the man (8:1c) recalls the opening line of the first movement, "O that he would kiss me with the kisses of his mouth" (1:2). The touch she desired, she now gives: "If I found you outside, I would kiss you." Moreover, in the beginning of the first section, she declared that his "love is better than wine" (1:2b, RSV), and at its end she reported that "he brought me to the *house* of wine" (2:4). Now, immediately after leading her lover to the *house* of her mother, she says:

> I would give you spiced wine to drink,
>> the juice of my pomegranates.
>>> (8:2, RSV)

These allusions to the introductory movement are confirmed by the ensuing words of the woman. They repeat verbatim her last statement in
the opening section:

> His left hand is under my head
>> and his right hand embraces me!
>>> (8:3)

With this description the woman ceases to address the man directly and
returns to the pattern of third-person narration that she has consistently
used at the end of all the preceding movements. Thus she wavers between
distance and intimacy.

Finally, the refrain of the fourth movement echoes, with variation,
the adjurations of the first and second. Though the gazelles and the hinds
of the fields are missing, the rhythm of love is again affirmed:

> I adjure you, O daughters of Jerusalem,
>> that you stir not up nor awaken love
>> until it please.
>>> (8:4, RSV)

Like the third and fourth movements, the fifth (8:5–14) begins with
a question. Perhaps the daughters ask it, since they similarly introduced
the fourth movement.

> Who is that coming up from the wilderness,
>> leaning upon her lover?
>>> (8:5, RSV*)

To conclude this unit, the woman speaks, as indeed she has done at the
close of each section. In all these instances, she has referred to the man
in the third person, though in the fourth movement she also addressed
him directly. In this final movement, however, distance and ambivalence
vanish altogether. Intimacy triumphs. The woman summons her man to
love:

> Make haste, my lover,
>> and be like a gazelle
> or a young stag
>> upon the mountains of spices.
>>> (8:14, RSV*)

No refrain of adjuration follows these closing words: with the consummation of Eros it is unnecessary. Thus, the daughters of Jerusalem disappear, and we, the readers, must also withdraw. Just as the first words of the woman at the very beginning of the Song invited us to enter the circle of intimacy (1:2a), so her last words deny us further participation. In the end she speaks directly and only to her lover, the bone of her bone and the flesh of her flesh. The man of Genesis 2 once left his father and mother to cleave to his woman (v. 24); now the woman of the Song bids her man make haste, and in this bidding all others are left behind. The circle of intimacy closes in exclusion when two become one.

As a symphony of love, the Song of Songs unfolds in five major movements: 1:2–2:7; 2:8–3:5; 3:6–5:8; 5:9–8:4; 8:5–14. The beginnings and endings of these sections demonstrate the interweaving of cyclic patterns in the overall structure. Through the convergence of form and content, these patterns recall cyclic designs throughout Genesis 2. Moreover, several themes in Genesis 2:21–24 have also enhanced our reading of this musical score: the creation and consummation of sexuality; an erotic poem; emphasis upon the female in the design of the literature; and the absence of God when female and male unite. Building upon this interpretation, let us explore leitmotifs within the Song of Songs that further reflect and elucidate Genesis 2–3.

EXPLORING VARIATIONS ON A THEME

A garden (*gan*) in Eden locates the tragedy of disobedience in Genesis 2–3. But the garden itself signals delight, not disaster, and that perspective reverberates in the Song of Songs. The woman is the garden (*gan*), and to the garden her lover comes. This vocabulary appears first in the third movement when the man describes love withheld:

> A garden locked is my sister, my bride,
> a garden locked, a fountain sealed.
> (4:12, RSV; cf. 4:15)

Immediately the woman responds, offering her garden to him:

> Awake, O north wind,
> and come, O south wind!
> Blow upon *my* garden,
> let its fragrance be wafted abroad.

> Let my lover come to *his* garden,
>   and eat its choicest fruits.
>   (4:16, RSV★; cf. 4:13)

The man accepts the invitation, claiming her garden as his own:

> I come to *my* garden, my sister, my bride (5:1a, RSV)

This imagery of intercourse continues in the fourth movement. Answering questions from the daughters of Jerusalem, the woman says:

> My lover has gone down to his garden,
>   to the beds of spices,
> to pasture in the gardens,
>   and to gather lilies.
>   (6:2, RSV★; cf. 6:11)

And in the fifth movement, the last words of the man address the woman with the same motif:

> O you who dwell in the gardens,
>   my companions are listening for your voice;
>   let me hear it.
>   (8:13, RSV)

Male and female first became one flesh in the Garden of Eden. There a narrator reported briefly their sexual union (Gen. 2:24). Now in another garden, the lovers themselves praise at length the joys of intercourse. Possessive adjectives do not separate their lives. "My garden" and "his garden" blend in mutual habitation and harmony. Even person and place unite: the garden of eroticism is the woman.

In this garden the sensuality of Eden expands and deepens. Emerging gradually in Genesis 2–3, all five senses capitulated to disobedience through the tasting of the forbidden fruit. Fully present in the Song of Songs from the beginning, these senses saturate the poetry to serve only love. Such love is sweet to the taste, like the fruit of the apple tree (2:3; cf. 4:16; 5:1, 13). Fragrant are the smells of the vineyards (2:13), the perfumes of myrrh and frankincense (3:6), the scent of Lebanon (4:11), and the beds of spices (5:13; 6:2). The embraces of lovers confirm the delights of touch (1:2; 2:3–6; 4:10, 11; cf. 5:1; 7:6–9; 8:1, 3). A glance of the eyes ravishes the heart (4:9; 6:13), as the sound of the lover thrills it (5:2). Taste, smell, touch, sight, and hearing permeate the garden of the Song.

Plants also adorn this place of pleasure—"every tree that is pleasant to the sight and good for food" (Gen. 2:9, RSV). Again, what the storyteller in Genesis reported succinctly, the voices in the Song praise extensively. They name not only the trees, but also the fruits and the flowers. For instance, in the first movement the woman describes herself to the man:

> I am a lotus of the plain,
>   a lily of the valleys.
>
>   (2:1)

The word *lily* suggests to the man an extravagant comparison, to which even the thorns and thistles of the earth (cf. Gen. 3:18) contribute:

> As a lily among brambles,
>   so is my love among women.
>   (2:2, RSV★)

The woman replies in kind:

> As an apple among the trees of the wood,
>   so is my lover among men.
>   (2:3a, RSV★)

Yet her comparison does not stop there. She expands upon images from the plant world to portray the joy her lover embodies:

> In his shadow I delight to rest
>   and his fruit is sweet to my taste.
> He brought me to the house of wine
>   and his emblem over me was love.
> Strengthen me with raisin cakes,
>   refresh me with apples,
> for faint with love am I.
>   (2:3b–5; cf. NAB [New
>   American Bible])

Throughout the Song of Songs other members of the plant world further specify "every tree pleasant to the sight and good for food": the mandrake (7:13), the fig tree (2:13), the pomegranate (4:3, 13; 6:7), the cedar (5:15), the palm (7:8), and "all trees of frankincense" (4:14, RSV). And among these many plants, no tree of disobedience grows (cf. Gen. 2:16–17). Instead, the lovers offer an open invitation to eat freely of every tree of the garden, as well as to drink from its fountain of delight. In their world of harmony, prohibition does not exist:

> Eat, O friends, and drink:
> drink deeply, O lovers!
>
> (5:1e, RSV)

The invitation to drink follows a description of the abundance of water that fills the garden:

> A garden fountain, a well of living water,
> and flowing streams from Lebanon.
>
> (4:15, RSV; cf. 4:12)

This imagery recalls the subterranean stream that watered the earth before creation (Gen. 2:6) and clearly invites comparison with the river flowing out of Eden to nourish that garden (Gen. 2:10–14). In both settings, food and water enhance life.

Animals as well inhabit these two gardens. In Genesis 2:18–20 their creation was marked with ambivalence. Closely identified with the earth creature, they were, nevertheless, a disappointment, for among them "was not found a companion fit for it." Indeed, the power which the earth creature exercised in naming the animals underscored their inadequacy for humankind. Yet, conversely, the animals provided a context for the joy of human sexuality. In Genesis 3, however, the ambivalence of their creation yielded completely to the villainous portrayal of the serpent. The most clever of all wild animals beguiled the naked couple to become their perpetual enemy (3:14). In the Garden of Eden, then, the animals lived in tension with the human creatures.

But in the garden of the Song of Songs this tension disappears. No serpent bruises the heel of female or male; no animals are indicted as unfit companions for humankind. To the contrary, the beasts of the field and the birds of the air (cf. Gen. 2:19) now become synonyms for human joy. Their names are metaphors for love. Scattered throughout the movements of the poetry, these creatures are often used for physical descriptions of the lovers. In the opening poem of the second movement, for example, the woman limns her mate:

> Leaping upon the mountains,
> bounding over the hills,
> My lover is like a gazelle,
> or a young stag.
>
> (2:8, 9a, RSV*; cf. 2:17b)

To these images she returns in the closing lines of the Song (8:14). In other places she compares her lover's black hair to a raven and his eyes to "doves beside springs of water" (5:11–12, RSV). Similarly, the man depicts the beauty of the woman in animal metaphors:

> Behold, you are beautiful, my love,
>   behold, you are beautiful!
> Your eyes are doves
>   behind your veil.
> Your hair is like a flock of goats,
>   moving down the slopes of Gilead.
> Your teeth are like a flock of shorn ewes
>   that have come up from the washing,
> Each having its twin,
>   and not one of them is bereaved.
>   (4:1–2, RSV*)
>
> . . . .
>
> Your two breasts are like two fawns,
>   twins of a gazelle,
>   that feed among the lilies.
>   (4:5, RSV; cf. 7:3)

The mare (1:9), the turtledove (2:12), and the lions and the leopards (4:8) also dwell in this garden where all nature extols the love of female and male. Clearly, the Song of Songs banishes the ambivalence toward animals that Genesis 2 introduced, just as it knows nothing of the villainous serpent in Genesis 3. Even the little foxes that spoil the vineyards can be captured by love (2:15). Thus, all animals serve Eros.

Work and play belong together in both the garden of creation and the garden of eroticism. To till and keep the Garden of Eden was delight until the primeval couple disobeyed, causing the ground to bring forth thorns and thistles and work to become pain and sweat (Gen. 2:15; 3:16, 18–19). In the first movement of the Song of Songs, the woman transforms the pain of work into pleasure. At the command of her mother's sons, she keeps vineyards under the scorching sun; yet, undaunted by this experience of forced labor, she associates it with play:

> The sons of my mother were angry at me;
>   they made me keeper of the vineyards.
> My own vineyard I have not kept!
>   (1:6, RSV*)

Identifying herself with a vineyard, the woman hints that her lover is *its*

keeper. Such playfulness directs her to the man, with another allusion to
work:

> Tell me, you whom my *nephesh* loves,
>   where do you pasture?
>
>   (1:7a)

The man may well be a shepherd, but for the woman his occupation is
the play of intercourse. After all, he pastures among the lilies (2:16; 6:3),
and she herself is a lily (2:1, 2). By analogy, the man is also a king (1:4,
12; 8:11, 12), but he neither rules nor dispenses wisdom. Instead, he
provides luxury for the sake of love. Hence, throughout the garden of
the Song, sexual play intertwines with work, redeeming it beyond the
judgments of Genesis 3:16–19.

Familial references offer still another study in contrasts. Although
in Genesis 2 the creation of male and female was totally independent of
parents, in the Song of Songs the births of the lovers are linked to their
mothers, though the fathers are never mentioned. Seven times, at least
once in every movement, the word *mother* appears in the poetry. The man
calls his love the special child of the mother who bore (*yld*) her (6:9),
even as the woman cites the travail of the mother who bore (*yld*) him
(8:5). Appropriately, both these references allude to the beauty of birth;
they know nothing at all of the multiplication of pain in childbearing (cf.
Gen. 3:16). Moreover, in yearning for closeness with her lover, the
woman wishes that he were a brother nursing at the breast of her mother
(8:1). Again, she parallels the desire for sexual union with her own conception; thus, she wants to lead the man

> into the house of my mother,
> and into the chamber of her
>   that conceived me.
>   (3:4; 8:2, RSV*)

This entry into the mother's house for intercourse suggests its opposite
in Genesis 2:24. There the man broke up a family for the sake of sexual
union. He left his father and mother to cleave to his woman. Standing
alone, without parents, the woman was highlighted as the one to whom
he must come. In the Song, the woman is emphasized, by contrast, as
the one who brings the man into her mother's house. From different
perspectives, two other passages in the Song also mention the mother.
The woman identifies her brothers as "sons of my mother" (1:6), and
later she beholds King Solomon

with the crown with which his mother crowned him
 on the day of his wedding,
 on the day of the gladness of his heart.
(3:11, RSV)

Unquestionably, these seven references to mother, without a single mention of father, underscore anew the prominence of the female in the lyrics of love. Once again, then, the Song of Songs expands and varies a theme present in Genesis 2–3.

 Belonging to a historical rather than a primeval setting, the Song also extends the witnesses to love beyond the human inhabitants of Eden. Certain groups are hostile, for not all the world loves a lover. Specifically, the woman encounters anger from her brothers (1:6) and physical assault from the watchmen of the city (5:7; cf. 2:3). But other witnesses celebrate the happiness and beauty of the lovers: kings (1:9; 3:7; 4:4); queens and concubines (6:8, 9); warriors (3:7; 6:4), indeed, an army with banners (6:4, 10); merchants with their fragrant powders (3:6); shepherds (1:7–8); and the daughters of Jerusalem. Moreover, the woman herself exults that other women, as well as men, adore her mate. In their attraction for him, she finds joy, not jealousy:

Your name is oil poured out;
 therefore, *the maidens* love you.
Draw me after you, let us make haste.
 The king has brought me into his chambers.
We will exult and rejoice in you;
 we will extol your love more than wine;
 rightly do *they* [masculine] love you.
(1:3b–4, RSV, italics mine)

Similarly, the man rejoices that other men, as well as women, delight in his partner:

O you who dwell in the gardens,
 my companions [masculine] are listening for your voice;
let me hear it.
(8:13, RSV)

. . . .

The maidens saw her and called her happy;
 the queens and concubines also, and they praised her.
(6:9b, RSV, italics mine)

Throughout the Song, Eros is inclusive; the love between two welcomes the love and companionship of many. Only at the end does exclusion close this circle of intimacy.

On two occasions (2:16; 6:3) the woman expresses intimacy by the formula "My lover is mine, and I am his." This interchange of pronouns parallels the union of "my garden" with "his garden" (4:16). Love is harmony. Neither male nor female asserts power or possession over the other. In light of Genesis 3:16, a third expression of this idea is particularly striking. The woman says, "I am my lover's and for me is his desire" (7:10). Her use of the word *desire* (t^e šûqâ) echoes, in contrast, the divine judgment upon the first woman: "Your desire [t^e šûqâ] shall be for your man, but he shall rule over you." In Eden, the yearning of the woman for harmony with her man continued after disobedience. Yet the man did not reciprocate; instead, he ruled over her to destroy unity and pervert sexuality. Her desire became his dominion. But in the Song, male power vanishes. His desire becomes her delight. Another consequence of disobedience is thus redeemed through the recovery of mutuality in the garden of eroticism. Appropriately, the woman sings the lyrics of this grace: "I am my lover's and for me is his desire."

A further hint of redemption comes in the way the word *name* is used in the two gardens. When the transformed earth creature called the woman 'iššâ (and himself 'îš), he did not name her but rather rejoiced in the creation of sexuality (Gen. 2:23). But when the disobedient man called his woman's *name* (šēm) Eve, he ruled over her to destroy their one flesh of equality (Gen. 3:20). On the other hand, the opening lines of the Song of Songs convert the motif of the name to the service of sexual fulfillment. The woman herself utters this word in a pun of adoration for the man:

> For better is your love than wine;
>   your anointing oils are fragrant;
> oil [š^e men] poured out is your *name* [š^e mekā].
>   (1:2b–3, RSV*)

Rather than following her man out of the garden (cf. Gen. 3:23–24), this woman bids him bring her to his palace of pleasure: "Draw me after you, let us make haste" (1:4, RSV). For her, naming is ecstasy, not dominion. A new context marks a new creation.

Love redeemed meets even death unflinchingly. Although the threat of death belonged to the creation of Eros (Gen. 2:17), it was through human disobedience that death became the disintegration of life. Harmony gave way to hostility; unity and fulfillment to fragmentation and dispersion. In the closing movement of the Song of Songs, this tragedy is reversed. Once again, eroticism can embrace the threat of death. The woman says:

> Let me be a seal upon your heart,
> Like the seal upon your hand.
> For love is fierce as death,
> Passion is mighty as Sheol;
> Its darts are darts of fire,
> A blazing flame.
>
> (8:6)

But she does more than affirm love as the equal of death. She asserts triumphantly that not even the primeval waters of chaos can destroy Eros:

> Many waters cannot quench love,
> neither can floods drown it.
> (8:7, RSV)

As a "garden fountain, a well of living water [*mayîm ḥayyîm*]" (4:5, RSV), a woman in love prevails over the many waters (*mayîm rabbîm*) of chaos. With such assurances, the poetry moves inexorably to its consummation.

COMPLETING THE SONG

Using Genesis 2–3 as a key for understanding the Song of Songs, we have participated in a symphony of love. Born to mutuality and harmony, a man and a woman live in a garden where nature and history unite to celebrate the one flesh of sexuality. Naked without shame or fear (cf. Gen. 2:25; 3:10), this couple treat each other with tenderness and respect. Neither escaping nor exploiting sex, they embrace and enjoy it. Their love is truly bone of bone and flesh of flesh, and this image of God male and female is indeed very good (cf. Gen. 1:27, 31). Testifying to the goodness of creation, then, eroticism becomes worship in the context of grace.

In this setting, there is no male dominance, no female subordination, and no stereotyping of either sex. Specifically, the portrayal of the woman defies the connotations of "second sex." She works, keeping vineyards and pasturing flocks. Throughout the Song she is independent, fully the equal of the man. Although at times he approaches her, more often she initiates their meetings. Her movements are bold and open: at night in the streets and squares of the city she seeks the one whom her *nephesh* loves (3:1–4). No secrecy hides her yearnings. Moreover, she dares to describe love with revealing metaphors:

> My lover put his hand to the latch,
>   and my womb trembled within me.
>   (5:4)

Never is this woman called a wife, nor is she required to bear children. In fact, to the issues of marriage and procreation the Song does not speak. Love for the sake of love is its message, and the portrayal of the female delineates this message best.

Though love is fulfilled when the woman and the man close the circle of intimacy to all but themselves (8:13–14), my imagination posits a postlude to the poetry. In this fantasy "the cherubim and a flaming sword" appear to guard the entrance to the garden of the Song (cf. Gen. 3:24). They keep out those who lust, moralize, legislate, or exploit. They also turn away literalists. But at all times they welcome lovers to romp and roam in the joys of eroticism:

> Arise, my love, my fair one,
>   and come away;
> for lo, the winter is past,
>   The rain is over and gone.
> The flowers appear on the earth,
>   the time of pruning has come,
> and the voice of the turtledove
>   is heard in our land.
> The fig tree puts forth its figs,
>   and the vines are in blossom;
>   they give forth fragrance.
> Arise, my love, my fair one,
>   and come away.
>   (2:10–13, RSV*)

The *Waṣf*

Marcia Falk

It is a paradox of human nature that strangeness, like its opposite, often breeds contempt. While the Song [of Songs] has been widely celebrated by Bible scholars and lay audiences alike, there is another mood, of uneasiness, even embarrassment, which sometimes murmurs beneath the din of our applause. This discontent seems to surface in discussions of a kind of passage in the Song known to Bible scholars as the *waṣf*. The scholarly investigations and treatments of the waṣf reveal some of the serious limitations of Bible scholarship in the realm of literary study, and expose, moreover, some of the prejudices most frequently applied to the Song as a whole. Primarily to shed light on these problems and to suggest solutions, including alternative ways to interpret the content of the Song, I treat the waṣf as a separate subject.

Waṣf, an Arabic word meaning "description," has come to refer to a kind of poem or poetic fragment that describes through a series of images the parts of the male and female body. While waṣfs are not uncommon in modern Arabic poetry, in ancient Hebrew literature they appear only in the Song of Songs. The similarity between certain passages in the Song and modern Arabic poems was discovered in the last century; because of this, the technical term *waṣf* has become familiar in scholarly studies of the Song.

Although the waṣf shares stylistic features with the rest of the Song, relying for poetic effect on parallelism, sound play, and the use of short rhythmic lines, it is formally stricter and more predictable than any other

From *Love Lyrics from the Bible: A Translation and Literary Study of the Song of Songs,* edited by David M. Gunn. © 1982 by the Almond Press.

material in the collection. Essentially a catalogue which describes in sequence, from top to bottom or bottom to top, segments of the male or female body, the waṣf appears, in part or in whole, in several different types of poem in the Song. Poem 15 is a love monologue with a partial waṣf; 19 is a composite which contains a complete waṣf; 20 is a love monologue which repeats some of the waṣf found in 15; and 22, framed as a dialogue, almost entirely comprises a complete waṣf [poems are appended at end of chapter]. Of these four, the waṣfs in poems 15, 20, and 22 are descriptions of a female, while the waṣf in 19 describes a male. To this last distinction and related issues I will return later.

Not only is the form of the waṣf fairly rigid and its subject matter determined at the outset, its treatment of the subject also follows a pattern: each part of the physique is described by means of specific, often unlikely images drawn from the realms of nature and artifice. While the imagery in the waṣf is usually visual, it sometimes appeals to other senses, as in the tactile "breasts like fawns" or the olfactory and tastelike associations of "lips like lilies."

It has been my observation that the imagery in the waṣfs is associated by English readers with the "peculiar" poetic characteristics of the Song and with the "exotic" nature of ancient Hebrew sensibility. (When giving readings of my translation, I find audiences particularly curious to hear how I rendered those strings of strange images known previously to them through the standard translations.) What is more difficult to understand, however, is the bewilderment of Bible scholars, who read the waṣfs in the original Hebrew and are familiar enough with texts of the ancient Near East not to consider ancient Hebrew literature exotic. Here are some typical examples of what these scholars say about the waṣfs:

> The comparison of the girl's hair to a flock of goats would have been straightforward and legitimate if mention of the slopes of Gilead had been omitted. As the image stands, the mountain background is, in reference to a girl's head, too large for the goats, for if they are bunched together there are too many slopes bare of goats, but if they are scattered the emphasis falls upon the girl's hairs rather than her hair. Thus the figure is bizarre, if not grotesque, possibly by intent of the author.
>
> (Leroy Waterman, *The Song of Songs: Translated and Interpreted as a Dramatic Poem*)

Only as playful banter can be rationally explained the grotesque description by the lover to the damsel of her neck as "like the tower of David built for an armoury," of her nose "as the tower of Lebanon which looketh toward Damascus," and of her head like mount Carmel (iv 4, vii 5, 6), and similar comical comparisons of her other limbs.

(M. H. Segal, "The Song of Songs,"
Vetus Testamentum 12 [1962])

To our sensibilities the images are admittedly comical and puzzling. Consequently, one must infer either that this was the poet's intention, in which case the *waṣfs* are not "descriptive love songs" at all but parodies, or that our perspective radically differs from the poet's.

(Richard N. Soulen, "The *Waṣfs* of the Song
of Songs and Hermeneutic," *Journal of
Biblical Literature* 86 [1967])

"Bizarre," "grotesque," "comical," "puzzling"—do these aptly describe the imagery in the Song? If so, what words might describe acclaimed passages in English literature such as the conceits of the metaphysical poets: for example, Crashaw's comparison in "The Weeper" of Mary Magdalene's tears to "two faithful fountains; / Two walking baths; two weeping motions; / Portable, and compendious oceans"; or Donne's two lovers like legs of a compass in "A Valediction: Forbidding Mourning"? And how shall we characterize the poetry of the modern age, including the imagism of writers like Pound, Moore, Williams, H. D.? Will it not seem odd to find poets comparing the inside of a subway station to a branch of a tree, as in Pound's famous two-line poem "In a Station of the Metro": "The apparition of these faces in the crowd; / Petals on a wet, black bough."? And how will we even begin to understand foreign literatures which make poetic statements like this one: "Inside of one potato / there are mountains and rivers."?

The point seems obvious: the difficulty resides not in the nature of the waṣfs but rather in the critical interpretation. The flaw is not in our text but in the failure of scholars to appreciate the very essence of metaphor, at the core of great poetry from many different eras and cultures. That essence is the extensive psychic association which the poet Robert Bly calls "leaping":

Thought of in terms of language, leaping is the ability to associate fast. In a great ancient or modern poem, the considerable distance between the associations, the distance the spark has to leap, gives the lines their bottomless feeling, their space, and the speed of the association increases the excitement of the poetry.

It is essentially this leap the metaphor makes—the leap between object and the image which describes it, that is, between tenor and vehicle—which troubles Bible scholars. Richard Soulen points out that a fault with scholarly interpretation lies with its literalistic approach. This seems right, especially if we understand literalism here to mean the need to find between tenor and vehicle a one-to-one correspondence in all details. So Waterman, in the passage quoted above, cannot accept the metaphor of hair like a flock of goats on a mountainside because the size of individual hairs in relation to the size of the head is not exactly in proportion to the relationship of size between goats and a mountain.

At the other extreme, however, Soulen proposes to eliminate all visualizable correspondence between tenor and vehicle, arguing that this is what T. S. Eliot had in mind when he spoke of "objective correlative." Soulen writes:

> Its [the *waṣf's*] purpose is not to provide a parallel to visual appearance or, as we shall see, primarily to describe feminine or masculine qualities metaphorically. The *tertium comparationis* must be seen instead in the feelings and sense experiences of the poet himself who then uses a vivid and familiar imagery to present to his hearers knowledge of those feelings in the form of art.

Soulen is right to note that the imagery in the waṣfs is vivid and familiar, for certainly it must have been so in the cultural context of its time. But he offers little to make it similarly vivid or familiar to us, since he declines to analyze it in its particulars, either unwilling or unable to find in it *particular* objective correlatives for emotional experience. Rather, he concludes

> that interpretation is most correct which sees the imagery of the *waṣf* as a means of arousing emotions consonant with those experiences by the suitor as he beholds the fullness of his beloved's attributes. . . . Just as the sensual experiences of love, beauty, and joy are vivid but ineffable, so the description which centers in and seeks to convey these very subjective feelings must for that reason be unanalytical and imprecise.

This is hardly a valid application of Eliot's principle, nor is it an accurate description of what poetry does, for it fails to address the question of *how* emotions are aroused in the reader—how, finally, the ineffable ideal is conveyed through words. By reducing the imagery in the waṣfs to vague evocation of ineffable feelings, Soulen deprives the relationship between tenor and vehicle of meaning. The point of comparison between a woman's hair and flocks of goats on a mountainside lies, for him, "simply in the emotional congruity existing between two beautiful yet otherwise disparate sights." But if this were so, the poet might have chosen any beautiful thing for an image; there would hardly be a point to interpreting this particular metaphor, or any other. Moreover, there would be no way to distinguish an apt metaphor from a poor one, here or in any text, for as long as tenor and vehicle had vaguely similar emotional associations, the metaphor would be valid.

But one expects more of good poetry, and the Song fulfills these expectations. In fact, the metaphors in the Song express a sophisticated poetic sensibility which, although foreign to us today, can be made accessible through critical analysis. The process is simply one of proper visualization—taking the right focus or perspective, making explicit the implicit context, filling in the unverbalized details. Take the image that has so perturbed the scholars: one can easily picture hair to be like goats on a mountainside by viewing the scene from a distance. From afar, the sight of goats winding down the slopes of the Israeli countryside is striking: the dark animals weave a graceful pattern against the paler background of the hills, suggesting dark waves of hair falling down a woman's back. Similarly, a herd of sheep, emerging fresh from the water, provides an ingenious metaphor when seen at a distance: the paired, white animals suggest twin rows of white teeth. If this seems contrived to our sensibilities, we should at least recognize that it is no more so than the Petrarchan convention of comparing teeth to pearls. In fact, most of the images in the waṣfs are no more difficult to visualize than the more familiar Petrarchan figures of speech found in Renaissance poetry. With probing, even the most abstruse images in the waṣfs open up to visualization. Take, for example, the forehead behind the veil, which is compared to a slice of pomegranate. It is puzzling only at first; after reflecting on it with the mind's eye, we see a gleam of red seeds through a net of white membrane. Might this not be like ruddy skin glimpsed through a mesh of white veil? Once we see the image, we realize that it is no more artificial nor less artful than the Petrarchan comparison of cheeks to roses.

It is unnecessary and unfortunate to dismiss the images in the waṣf as either bizarre or imprecise. Meaningful interpretation lies between these extremes, in nonliteralistic visualization. Thus in translating the waṣfs, when an image depended upon familiarity with a foreign landscape, I sometimes suggested vantage points or settings so that modern English readers would see in it what the original audience might have seen. Where the King James states, "Thy hair is as a flock of goats, that appear from mount Gilead," I rendered, "Your hair—as black as goats / winding down the slopes," hinting at color and contour where they might otherwise be missed. For the same reason I often eliminated proper place names and substituted descriptions, as here in "the slopes" for "mount Gilead," and, in another waṣf, "two silent pools" for "pools in Heshbon," "the hills" for "Damascus," "majestic mountain" for "Carmel." When an image was not primarily visual, I tried to indicate its specific sensory appeal, as in "Lips like lilies, sweet / And wet with dew." Occasionally, to keep a metaphor from sounding hackneyed, I introduced a new detail, as in "Hair in waves of black / Like wings of ravens." Although wings are not mentioned in the original, neither is it likely that the Hebrew phrase "black as a raven" was, in its time, the cliché that it has become in English.

Thus the method of interpretative visualization led me often to lines which differ from those in the standard translations. My goal was to let the images be vivid rather than puzzling pictures of a foreign but accessible culture, in hopes that the imagery of the Song might eventually be demystified for both scholarly and general audiences.

A related literary issue which has been raised specifically in connection with the waṣf, but which has ramifications for our understanding of the Song as a whole, is the topic of male and female roles and representations in the Song, and their conformity to stereotypes. One quotation from Soulen should help illuminate the serious problems in scholarly interpretation of this question:

> The poetic imagination at work in 5:10–16 where the maiden speaks of her lover is less sensuous and imaginative than in the *waṣfs* of chapters 4 and 7. This is due in part to the limited subject matter and may even be due to the difference in erotic imagination between poet and poetess.

Now let us look once more at the text. A brief glance at the waṣf in 5:10–16 (my poem 19) reveals that it is no less sensuous and imaginative than any of the other waṣfs. Soulen's evaluation, then, perhaps derives from a preconception that the description of a man's body, as opposed to a woman's, is necessarily "limited subject matter." Indeed, such a preconception is not surprising in a culture where men are trained to assume that exaltation of male beauty is frivolous at best, embarrassing at worst. With such bias, any attempt to describe or praise the male body is doomed to fail. However, this bias was hardly embedded in the poetic imagination of the original text: there is nothing at all embarrassed or limited about the female voice speaking the waṣf. And this voice, of course, may have been created by either a male or female poet. The deduction of a "poetess" behind a female persona is not only naive but surprising in its context, because Soulen, like most scholars, talks in general about the author of the Song as male. There is a double prejudice at work here. On the one hand Soulen speaks of the poet as masculine throughout the essay, seeming to disregard the possibility that women contributed to the authorship of the text. On the other hand, when faced with a description of male beauty, he assumes that the passage was composed by a female, at which point he dismisses it as inferior and not warranting further study. (The quoted statement comes from a footnote; Soulen never even mentions this waṣf again in his text.) Finally, he assumes that poets and poetesses have different (levels of? qualities of?) "erotic imagination." The imagination of the poetess is, for Soulen, not just "different" but inferior; it is the possible cause of a less lively poem.

Soulen's attitude toward the text is hardly unique; on the contrary, it is representative of much modern scholarship. But no matter how common this attitude, we should recognize that it derives from specific, culture-bound prejudices which are incompatible with the cultural sensibility that created the Song, a text that offers a thoroughly nonsexist view of heterosexual love. As is apparent in many poems in the Song, women speak as assertively as men, initiating action at least as often; so too, men are free to be as gentle, as vulnerable, and even as coy as women. Men and women are similarly praised by each other for their sensuality and beauty, not only in the waṣfs but throughout the Song. As another Bible scholar, Phyllis Trible, has eloquently demonstrated, the Song affirms and celebrates mutuality; in it "there is no male dominance, no female subordination, and no stereotyping of either sex."

Sexist interpretation of the waṣf, and of the Song in general, is a striking example of how the text can be distorted by culturally biased reading. To interpret the Song authentically, we must shed the cultural blinders that make what is foreign seem strange. It may even turn out that this ancient text has something new to teach us about how to redeem sexuality and love in our fallen world.

Poem 15

How fine
you are, my love,
your eyes like doves'
behind your veil

Your hair—
as black as goats
winding down the slopes

Your teeth—
a flock of sheep
rising from the stream
in twos, each with its twin

Your lips—
like woven threads
of crimson silk

A gleam of pomegranate—
your forehead
through your veil

Your neck—
a tower
adorned with shields

Your breasts—
twin fawns
in fields of flowers

Until
the day is over,
shadows gone,

I'll go
up to the hills
of fragrant bloom

How fine
you are, my love,
my perfect one

Poem 19

I sleep, but my heart stirs,
restless,
        and dreams . . .

My lover's voice here, at the door—

Open, my love, my sister,
my dove, my perfect one,
for my hair is soaked with the night.

Should I get up, get dressed, and dirty my feet?

My love thrusts his hand at the latch
and my heart leaps for him.
I rise to open for my love,
my hands dripping perfume on the lock.
I open, but he has gone.

I run out after him, calling, but he is gone.

The men who roam the streets,
guarding the walls,
beat me and tear away my robe.

O women of the city,
Swear to me!
If you find my lover
You will say
That I am sick with love.

Who is your love
And why do you bind us by oath?

My love is radiant
As gold or crimson,
Hair in waves of black
Like wings of ravens.

Eyes like doves, afloat
Upon the water,

Bathed in milk, at rest
On brimming pools.

Cheeks like beds of spices,
Banks of flowers,
Lips like lilies, sweet
And wet with dew.

Studded with jewels, his arms
Are round and golden,
His belly smooth as ivory,
Bright with gems.

Set in gold, his legs,
Two marble columns—
He stands as proud as cedars
In the mountains.

Man of pleasure—sweet
To taste his love!
Friend and lover chosen
For my love.

Beautiful woman,
Where has your lover gone to?
Where has he gone?
We'll help you look for him.

My love has gone to walk
Within his garden—
To feed his sheep and there
To gather flowers.

I turn to meet my love,
He'll turn to me,
Who leads his flock to feed
Among the flowers.

Poem 20

Striking as Tirza
        you are, my love,
Bright as Jerusalem,

frightening as visions!
Lower your eyes
for they make me tremble

Your hair—as black as goats
winding down the slopes
Your teeth—a flock of sheep
rising from the stream
in twos, each with its twin
A gleam of pomegranate—
your forehead through your veil

Sixty queens, eighty brides,
endless numbers of women—
One is my dove, my perfect one,
pure as an only child—
Women see her
and sing of her joy,
Queens and brides
chant her praise

Who is she? staring
down like the dawn's eye,
Bright as the white moon,
pure as the hot sun,
Frightening as visions!

Poem 22

Dance for us, princess, dance,
as we watch and chant!

What will you see as I move
in the dance of love?

Your graceful, sandalled feet,
Your thighs—two spinning jewels,
Your hips—a bowl of nectar
brimming full

Your belly—golden wheat
Adorned with daffodils,

Your breasts—two fawns, the twins
    of a gazelle

Your neck—an ivory tower,
Your eyes—two silent pools,
Your face—a tower that overlooks
    the hills

Your head—majestic mountain
Crowned with purple hair,
Captivating kings
    within its locks

Beauty and the Enigma

Francis Landy

> *Denn das Schöne ist nichts*
> *als des Schrecklichen Anfang, den wir noch grade ertragen,*
> *und wir bewunden es so, weil es gelassen verschmäht,*
> *uns zu zerstören.*

> *(For Beauty's nothing*
> *but beginning of Terror we're still just able to bear,*
> *and why we adore it so is because it serenely disdains*
> *to destroy us.)*
>
> RILKE, *Duino Elegies* 1

In essence this chapter is a close reading of four of the most difficult passages of the Song [of Songs], endeavouring to show that the difficulty, far from being an insuperable obstacle, is in fact part of the meaning, and contributes greatly to its beauty. The four episodes, symmetrically situated at opposite extremities of the Song, are linked through close correspondences of imagery and thematic material. The relationship of the ambiguity of the Song to its beauty and the ambivalence of love will be the principal subject of enquiry.

Critics have been quick to note the beauty of the Song, but few have made any attempt either to analyse it, or to consider it as an integral part of its composition. They ignore it as purely decorative, and turn to more serious matters. Similarly, while individual ambiguities, paronomasias, and so on have received attention, they have not been perceived as more than an occasional device, or rhetorical ornament. Pope links the ideas

From *Paradoxes of Paradise: Identity and Difference in the Song of Songs,* edited by David M. Gunn. © 1983 by the Almond Press.

of Beauty and Terror, but in a mythological context. For him the Beloved is simply a manifestation of the black, beautiful, passionate, bloodthirsty, venereal and virginal goddess who appears everywhere under different names—Anat, Ishtar, Kali in India, the Black Madonna in Europe, the Shekhinah in the Kabbalah. What is not clear is whether he regards this as the literal meaning, and therefore the Song as a cultic poem dedicated to a demonic goddess, or whether it is a subliminal paradigm. This is because he never escapes from his fascination for the arcane and primitive, never extracts from it its human meaning. Beauty and Terror are externalised as attributes of ancient mysteries, instead of being comprehended as very intimate feelings.

Albert Cook, too, has alluded to this relationship, somewhat cryptically and indecisively. At one point he seems to regard Beauty and Terror as alternatives: the Beloved *chooses* to love rather than to terrorise; at another, love apparently appropriates terror. But nowhere does he treat Beauty and Terror as more than a chance conjunction.

The most sensitive interpreter of the aesthetics of the Song is Leo Krinetzki, who pays a great deal of attention in his earlier commentary to its alliterative patterns and their possible significance; for the most part his observations consist, however, of simple impressionistic correspondences that do not affect the Song's intrinsic meaning. It is unfortunate that this preoccupation with word-music does not appear in his later work. He recognises, commenting on chapter 6, verse 4, the association of Beauty and Terror as corresponding to the Good and Terrible Mother respectively. It would be interesting to correlate, on a sophisticated level, sound values, for example, synaesthesia with his now Jungian interpretation.

H. P. Müller also has a passing mention of the coupling of Beauty and Terror in 6:4 and 6:10, as divine attributes projected onto the Beloved; it does not however figure greatly, as it could, in his analysis of the transformation of mythic speech and lyric speech, of beauty in the service of the divine.

Beauty in the Song is an all-pervasive quality that one cannot separate from the love of the lovers, the world they inhabit, or the language in which the poem is written. The three levels signify each other: the beauty of the lovers parallels that of the world, and both are expressed, exist only through the speech that describes them. Moreover, this beauty is contagious, passes from one level to another. Lyricism persuades us to accept the possibility of this beauty, because we imagine it emanates from a supreme inspiration; a golden language imitates a golden age. At the same time it confers its gold on that age. Similarly, we are persuaded of the beauty of the lovers through their comparison with beautiful things; but equally their metaphorical equivalents are graced through association with the lovers, they acquire a human beauty. For instance, when the Beloved is compared to Jerusalem and Tirzah, we learn something about Jerusalem and Tirzah as well as the Beloved.

The beauty the Song celebrates is very powerful, and consequently frightening, as we have found in the last chapter; a king is caught in its trammels in 7:6; the heart is overwhelmed in 4:9. In 6:4, the verse I have just cited, the comparison of the Beloved with the beauty of Jerusalem and Tirzah is followed by the mystifying "'ayummâ kannidgālôt (terrible as constellations,)" and the plea "Turn your eyes away from me, for they dazzle me." This in turn reflects the contrary impulses towards fusion and differentiation, self-surrender and self-possession.

Poetry depends on ambiguity for its richness. A poem is a counterpoint of multiple meanings, its essence is "multiplex, polysemantic," as Jakobson says. The discussion [elsewhere] amply illustrates the depth of symbolic association in the Song. Critics who confine themselves to a flat, one-dimensional interpretation, a paraphrase in other words, consequently err as greatly as allegorical expositors, who substituted a spiritual for its carnal meaning. For love is of infinite significance. Everything in the poem is implicated in the love of the lovers; for example, Jerusalem and Tirzah are its subject, as well as the Beloved. Human love is part of the fertility of nature, and both are expressed through the love of language.

The love of the world, man and language correspond to each other in the Song through metaphor; they also implicate each other. Language preserves all that is left of the poet, his characters, and his world; as a sexual metaphor, it is an intercourse of vocables; in it, the world finds expression. The lovers create the poem out of their love; they care for and cultivate nature, the gardens and vineyards of the Song, just as they cultivate speech, loving the world, finding words for it, using it to describe their love. Nature pervades language sensually, as sound; its fruit, honey, and so on, sustains the lovers, and reproducing itself "after its kind" it sympathetically stimulates them; they are part of the spring.

The language combines two main functions, the *intellectual* function and the *emotive* one. The *intellectual* function refers to the analysis of the phenomenology of love; on the natural level, this manifests itself in what one might term "a grammar of the senses." The emotive function calls for the reader's participation in the experience of the lovers, his empathy.

Ideally, the *signifiant* is identified with the *signifié,* the world of the poem is sensuously apprehended in its word. Thus the poem is a *synthesis* of the three levels we distinguished, language, man and nature; its basic form is metaphor. As more and more words are found to be equivalent, so does the poem come to be a tautology.

For this reason, a feeling of paradox pervades all the language of the Song. Fundamentally, it attempts the impossible: to communicate in language what is beyond language. Language is an intermediary, temporal and physical, while love is a fusion beyond speech. Moreover, direct experience cannot be expressed in language, yet poetry—all poetry—tries to recreate sensations, to make words "say" something, as well as signifying it. Hence the language of the Song is very difficult when one tries to comprehend it intellectually, and very simple and compulsive if one engages in it with one's feelings. This paradox is analogous to that of love, that two can become one and yet remain distinct. The relationship of language and the world reflects, too, the paradoxical status of man, who is both natural and cultural, part of nature and apart from it.

At this point we may make a distinction between an ambiguity and an enigma. An enigma may be defined as a negative ambiguity. Whereas an ambiguity has a double meaning, an enigma arises from an unanswered question. It occurs wherever speech is reticent. Ambiguities, however, frequently generate enigmas, whenever they result in a puzzling contradiction. Between the horns of a paradox dwells an enigma.

Within the limits of its paradoxes the Song is wholly enigmatic. We never know quite what happens or whether anything happens, and all the anecdotal energy that we devote to the construction of the narrative results either in false solutions, or in frustration. There is no single truth in the poem, only an inexpressible reality. Yet the poem tempts our imaginative, constructive efforts through its prodigality with clues, the promise of the brilliant fragments of narrative that compose it. Even these little dream-sequences, however, are riddled with doubts and ambiguities. They rarely have a beginning and an end, are reminiscent of snatches of radio plays that one switches on and off. They modulate the one to the other abruptly, without transition. Internally, they often turn on key double-meanings which, when examined, are found to derive from the central paradoxes. We will be looking at some of these in due course.

The enigma then is a feature of the narrative code of the poem, its dynamic forward movement that always turns back on itself, becomes timeless. On the other hand, its ambiguities are a set of concomitant meanings, synchronic processes. Movement in stillness, stillness in movement are the recurrent subjects of poetry, the "real place for wonder," as Northrop Frye puts it. He continues that the mystery of the poem does not emanate from "something unknown or unknowable in the poem, but something unlimited within it." I confess I do not quite understand this, for the unlimited is surely always unknowable. In "great poems," however, the mystery becomes as manifest as possible, somehow finds expression, without thereby becoming the less mysterious. The great poet never lets the mystery alone. To adapt Wittgenstein's formulation, the poet always speaks where he should be silent.

Beauty can only be experienced at a distance, in objects contemplated separately from oneself, preserved intact and ineffable. Thus Beauty is always the result of tension between desire and control, instinctual energy and repression. In its pure form the desire is to unite with, to integrate, to destroy the otherness of the other. It can be dangerous, expressing itself, for example, in the rite of "sparagmos," the rending of the living body. Yet it is essential to life. Hence the ambivalence of Beauty, as the object of desire. Because men project their emotions onto the source of arousal, the destructive, sadistic impulses evoked by Beauty are attributed to Beauty itself. It is Beauty that causes men to "lose their heads," and is responsible for dangerous explosions of irrational feeling. One might say—a popular myth concerning rape or sadism—that the victim deserves what she gets, for she provokes it through her very presence. Then the beautiful woman becomes the bad woman, the temptress, mingling polarities of adoration, fear, and fascinated contempt.

Ugliness is in fact not very far from Beauty, as Anton Ehrenzweig has argued with an abundance of examples. Aesthetic values are extraordinarily volatile. For Ugliness is a rejection of the elements that Beauty disguised. Beauty becomes ugly when it is too threatening, too terrible. The most awe-inspiring works of art are those where the tension is greatest, the ugliness most nearly unbearable (e.g., *King Lear*), and the aesthetic triumph consequently most breathtaking.

Man is fatefully attracted by mystery, for he seeks in it his ultimate answer. Hence the profusion of mystery cults and oracular utterances. Yet he also fears it, because the ultimate mystery is death. Knowledge is thus acutely perilous, for it promises an integration of good and evil, a mastery over chaos. For this reason knowledge carries with it a sense of beauty. It is a rhythmical alternation of an intense curiosity, which is but one manifestation of the erotic drive, with an ability to stand back and perceive a whole object. We can now see the relationship of ambiguity and ambivalence, meaning and value; for it is meaning that one most values. Ambiguity always arouses feelings of ambivalence, for it both conceals and reveals; this is true even when it is relatively empty of emotive content, as in trivial puns. When it expresses conflict or unsuspected depth, aesthetic admiration is stirred by the integration of different psychic levels, the successful formulation, at a distance, of intimate disturbances. The ambiguity enables unacknowledged subversive wishes to be fulfilled surreptitiously, often through heavy disguise. Octavio Paz, for example, has pointed out the metaphorical link between *anus* and *sun* in Spanish Gongoresque poetry.

Beauty then becomes enigmatic, and not only because of the unanswered question, "Will she be mine or not?" This merely expresses it in practical terms. It is enigmatic because of the powerful charge of repressed feeling, the wish to destroy it and the wish to preserve it. Beauty is thus very close to mystery, which knowledge seeks to penetrate. Mystery is beautiful when it is not terrible. Beauty is never very far from Death either, for we long to humanise what we most fear.

First Episode: 1:5–6

שְׁחוֹרָה אֲנִי וְנָאוָה בְּנוֹת יְרוּשָׁלָ͏ִם כְּאָהֳלֵי קֵדָר כִּירִיעוֹת שְׁלֹמֹה׃
אַל־תִּרְאֻנִי שֶׁאֲנִי שְׁחַרְחֹרֶת שֶׁשֱׁזָפַתְנִי הַשָּׁמֶשׁ בְּנֵי אִמִּי נִחֲרוּ־בִי
שָׂמֻנִי נֹטֵרָה אֶת־הַכְּרָמִים כַּרְמִי שֶׁלִּי לֹא נָטָרְתִּי׃

([1:5] I am black and comely, O daughters of Jerusalem, as the tents of Kedar, as the curtains of Solomon.
[6] Do not look on me, that I am dark, that the sun has burnt me; my mother's sons were angry with me; they made me a keeper of the vineyards; my own vineyard I did not keep.)

Stripped of explanations and comparisons, the passage consists of two clauses:

1. I am black and comely
2. Do not look on me

With the first the Beloved announces herself, to the reader as well as to the daughters of Jerusalem. In fact, for them words are superfluous; her beauty speaks for her, calls attention to itself. And what does she/it say? "Do not look on me!"

This presentation and withdrawal is not only pointless; it is para-doxical because Beauty is essentially something to be looked at, only exists in the eyes of the beholder. Furthermore, one normally introduces oneself to initiate conversation, in this case, the dialogue of the poem, but her extreme shyness, self-effacement—especially when the whole poem is dedicated to the vision of the Beloved—is the reverse of socia-bility.

Both clauses, too, are wholly enigmatic:

1. The conjunction wĕ in "I am black *and* comely" may also mean *but*. She may be a dark beauty or a beauty in spite of her darkness.
2. Her embarrassment is caused by her darkness, but is this enviable or contemptible, ugly or beautiful?

The alternatives are linked to each other; if we think of darkness as antithetical to beauty, we suppose hers to be a fear of contempt; if they are complementary, it is of the malice of envy.

Envy and contempt are in fact dialectically related, in two ways. One is simple and secondary; contempt is a defence against envy, where-with one comforts oneself, like the fox in the fable, by pretending that the other is not admirable. The other way is fundamental: that envy makes one wish either to emulate the other or, if that is impossible, to destroy the other; envy is the source of the most bitter hatred, one of whose weapons is disgust. The envied object becomes the pariah. These apparently contradictory functions reinforce each other, to ensure that envy is always accompanied by denigration.

Similarly, the paradox that Beauty says "Do not look on me" in fact expresses its essential ambivalence, as the product of desire and repres-sion. What it shows can only be seen indirectly.

To quote the epigraph, "Beauty is the beginning of terror we are still just able to bear" because it is a guise (vision, "gestalt") dolling up what we cannot bear to see—our naked anger, frenzy, greed. Beauty is a neutralisation of terror, imposing on it shape and structure, articulating it—finding words as guises for gazer and gazed—to exorcise it. Whether the Beloved is beautiful or ugly, humiliated or adored, depends on the success of this process, which is, in fact, a filter. "Throughout the ages almost everyone who has asked for literary clarity has actually been asking for a moderation of light, in order to protect the retina from shock, within a routine penumbra" (Lopez Velarde). Ugliness and Beauty, like envy and contempt, are linked terms, twin aspects of the aesthetic process, psychic distance—"I am black and comely."

In the Pastoral, courtly tradition, darkness of skin is ambivalent, while the conventional beauty is fair. Hence the synonym in English. A white complexion is delicate, unspoilt; and readily merges with the symbolism of whiteness as purity. The unspoilt, delicate girl is virginal, carefully raised within society to await her husband. The dark girl—whether Theocritus's "sunburnt Syrian," Virgil's Amyntas or Menalcas, or the "nut brown maid"—is available, and consequently less idealised and more enticing.

In our passage, conventional fair beauty is represented by the daughters of Jerusalem whom the beloved addresses, since she is conspicuous among them; it is the beauty of the city, of civilisation. The Beloved comes from outside "society"; her darkness is an index of class, like an accent. It is caused by sunburn, and rustic toil (1:6). For this reason it inspires contempt. But if it is beautiful, it is also enviable.

This envy is at the root of the Pastoral that accomplishes, in an innocuous, dreamlike setting, a complete inversion of social values. In the Pastoral, envy is creative, expressing a longing for identification, and a real empathy. The Beloved, with her dark beauty, signifies the hidden longing of the daughters of Jerusalem.

For if theirs is civilised beauty, hers is natural beauty, associated with sun and soil, and change. It incarnates in man the beauty of creation, and is the evidence of our intrinsic perfection. Civilisation, founded in repression, resists this faith, without which it would have no validity. As the amoral, uncivilised Beauty, the Beloved stands for the integration of good and evil, the totality of man and the world. She is thus the living presence of the irresponsible, untamed part of the daughters of Jerusalem. One may illustrate this by imagining their social situation; then the Beloved becomes a wish-fulfilling image of freedom and sexual license, activity and open spaces, of all of which they are deprived, enclosed in the city.

Her dark beauty is threatening because it is seductive, despised and worshipped for the same reason. Provoking sexual desire, it is the irreductible enemy of common sense, that says "Deceptive is charm, vain is beauty" (Prov. 31:30). It negates moral codes and political hierarchies; to refer to the royal persona, a king may fall in love with a country girl, who is worth his capital cities, Jerusalem and Tirzah. This subversiveness is characteristic of the Pastoral that idealises the rustic, uncorrupted by civilisation; for it thereby charms away, and ironically confirms, the reality of the peasant, his poverty, exploitation, coarseness, and incipient hostility. Peasants are usually discontented; the Pastoral, if taken literally, incites revolution.

The split-off self threatens a similar revolution within the daughters of Jerusalem. Virginity protects the self against intrusion; it remains a preserve and a mystery. Its corollary is the collective pride of the daughters of Jerusalem, and their concealed individuality. It expresses the fear of the one fate that is really worse than death: the loss of one's identity. However, erotic desire threatens to overwhelm this carefully brought-up, demure integrity, to submerge one self in the other, with rapturous abandon.

The two types of beauty, fair and dark, city and country, may now be identified with what Nietzsche describes as the Apollonian and Dionysiac poles of the aesthetic experience. The Dionysiac urge, subversive, irrepressible, is contained by Olympian detachment, psychic distance. The rest of my comments on our phrase "I am black and/but comely" will explore the implications of this tension as it relates to the Beloved and the daughters of Jerusalem.

If darkness of complexion is an index of class, and explicitly linked with the opposition of the country and city, this is not its total symbolic meaning. Darkness is a very powerful signifier, attached to our earliest memories. To begin with, it evokes the colour of the soil, and superimposes on the country/city dichotomy that of nature and culture. It is an obvious extension of the paradigm that the country girl should speak for the earth on which she works and with which she is in constant communion, as that the city girl should speak for the civilisation in which she has been raised. Furthermore, the identification of the Beloved with the earth is confirmed repeatedly within the text of the poem, through the metaphorical association of her body with landscapes and harvests. As an idea, an essential attribute of the earth is fertility, that expresses itself in man through the sexual drive. The dalliance of the lovers is one aspect of vernal excitement. Mythologically, in the Bible, the earth is the mother, from which the human race is formed (Gen. 2:7), and from which it feeds. Likewise, as we have seen throughout the poem, the Beloved is associated with a mother-figure (e.g., Song of Songs 3:4, 11; 8:2, 5).

We are absorbed in the mother in the womb, our first darkness. The light/dark antinomy is associated with the cycle of night and day, consciousness and unconsciousness, life and death. In the darkness we cannot distinguish self and other. The Dionysiac impulse, according to

Nietzsche, is the release of Thanatos, the will-to-die, to revert to a primordial undifferentiation, an oceanic pleroma. This is because Death is the concomitant of Life as *process,* the earthly/maternal cycle of decay and richness. Darkness, earth, fertility and decay recall ineluctably a most emotive process, excretion. Anal disgust is coupled with aesthetic idealisation in the creative work of the body. At the epicentre of explosive pleasure and extreme repression, defecation combines with genital sexuality and Dionysiac dissipation to form one pole of the aesthetic experience, the Dark Beloved. In contrast, the daughters of Jerusalem stand for a conservative civilisation, that excludes, for example, the vitality and subversive restlessness of the "lower classes." All its energies are devoted to its self-preservation, to a resistance to change and mortality (cf. city walls, soldiers, manners, agriculture). The daughters of Jerusalem attempt not to embark on life, so as to escape inevitable shipwreck.

The polarity may be formulated in the opposition of two terms that are usually held to be interchangeable: purity and innocence. *Purity* implies impurity, an already corrupted world. The fair daughters of Jerusalem, untouched by the sun, are fearful, since to the pure all things are impure. *Innocence,* however, precedes good and evil, in the garden, for instance; its ambivalence is in fact integration.

The relationship of the Beloved with the daughters of Jerusalem is an important structural element in the poem. From being an uncertain and casteless outsider she becomes the leader of their circle. She advises them, speaks for natural, spontaneous love; and when she is humiliated by the guardians of public morality (5:7), they aid her and comfort her, calling her "the most beautiful among women." If, as Northrop Frye claims, comedy is essentially characterised by social cohesion, this induction presents the cooperation of country and city, Thanatos and Eros, innocence and purity, and all the contraries we have cited, in mutual dependence.

The Dionysiac character of the Beloved may be further illustrated by a glance at Marvin Pope's list of mythological prototypes: Black Madonnas, virgin goddesses, Anat, Ishtar, Kali and so on that combine homicidal glee with an insatiable sexual appetite, to be the subject of dangerous adoration, at the centre of cultic circles.

With the images "as the tents of Kedar, as the curtains of Solomon" the Beloved supposedly illustrates her dark beauty; but in fact they draw attention away from it. The artifice of language disguises her challenge and reinforces her plea to be admitted into civilised society; part of the persuasiveness and reassurance of the Pastoral is imparted by the fiction that countryfolk speak mellifluously. But as ornamentation, the images surreptitiously widen the symbolic discourse of beauty and terror, at one remove.

The tents of Kedar are black and rich in the waterless desert; a chromatic correlation reinforced by a pun (*Kēdar: black*). But the simile works mainly through contextual connotation, a comparison of the situation of the Bedouin and that of the Beloved. Like her, they are exposed to the fierceness of the sun, and, like her, they are strangers to urban civilisation, subject to contempt and admiration. They are a menace, as raiders, and therewith virilely attractive, endowed with simple, tough virtues. The idealisation of nomads, free of the taint of civilisation, appears, for example, in Jeremiah's description of the Rechabites, and the general prophetic interplay of desert and settled land, ancient faithfulness and contemporary perversion. Thus it adds to the Pastoral opposition of country and city that of desert and fertility, an amplification that is in fact subversion for city and country are now one unit:

$$\text{City} \,/\, \text{Country} : (\text{City} + \text{Country}) \,/\, \text{Desert}.$$

The country, personified in the country girl, is compared with the desert, and yet is aligned against it. Through cultivation, the fields emerge from the desert, just as life comes from death. The Beloved thus mediates between the city and the wilderness. In the same way, the nomads are those who are able to survive, and indeed grow rich (cf. Isa. 21:16; Ezek. 27:21) in the desert, who can colonise the wilderness, through the shelter of their tents, their darkness. Thus the image combines the threat of destruction (raiders, desert, non-nature) with the hope of integration (virtue, innocence, humanisation).

The curtains of Solomon are at the opposite extreme. They are a metonymy for his palace, and hence for the beauty and splendour of his kingdom. They isolate the king as an individual behind the manifestations of his power, sexual and political; yet he is at the centre of society, the object of all its attentions. Moreover, it is especially the enigmatic inaccessible person who is attractive, the source of sexual intoxication.

Extremes meet. Both king and nomad are in some sense unconstrained by society and its laws, representing an irresponsible freedom; both mingle polarities of fear and romantic desire. This symmetrical opposition to the daughters of Jerusalem, as well as their syntagmatic coupling as images for the Beloved, establishes a hidden link, on a geographical axis (desert—country—city—palace), parallel to the transformation of the Beloved from rural outsider to leader of the circle, and royal mistress.

The attributes common to Solomon and Kedar are those that essentially characterise dark beauty, with its Dionysiac ambivalence, coming from outside society, incarnated and worshipped within it. Yet the Beloved is not like Solomon, but merely like his curtains, defined in terms of the other. She is the mediator, in other words, between the king and the kingdom, between the desert and man.

Chapter 1, verse 6, explains the Beloved's bashfulness by means of a story: "Do not look on me, that I am black, that the sun has scorched me; my mother's sons were angry with me; they made me a keeper of vineyards; my own vineyard I did not keep." The enigma is displaced, first synchronically, through simile, and now diachronically, through narrative. Like the comparisons, the anecdote entertains the listeners, rhetorically seduces them; they unconsciously obey her command, not to look on her. The paradoxical state is accounted for, but only in terms of paradoxical events. Events supposedly speak for themselves; hence the Beloved appeals to an objective but confused authority, exposing society's double-mindedness, its own ambivalence.

Historically contempt/envy turns into persecution; the Beloved fears rejection because she has so much suffered it. She is driven out of her family, tormented by the sun, and even exiled from herself—"my own vineyard I did not keep." Yet she is made the keeper of the vineyards! The wry irony of the sequence turns on this transformation of the neglect of one's own vineyard into the care of others, of the rejection by the brothers into social responsibility. In the Song wine is a recurrent sexual metaphor; grapes are the fruit of Dionysus, tended by the intoxicating Beloved. The metaphorical equivalence of sex and alcohol, vagina and vine, makes her the source of drunkenness, the seductive sorceress, ever-available and by the same token abandoned, both by herself and by her family. Sociologically, forsaken women are both exploited by society and excluded from it; in terms of the Pastoral, the tender of grapes works to free others of care, to make society irresponsible and light-headed.

The sun that ripens the grapes burns the woman; through its virulence the rage of the brothers becomes a cosmic violence. Yet it is because of this combined malevolence that she is darkly beautiful, as the victim of the sadistic cycle, attraction through hatred. Stranger still, the sun, the source of light and splendour, causes darkness in women, while the daughters of Jerusalem are fair, because they have been shielded from it. There is thus a correlation between the city, to which she says, "Do not look on me," and the intent gaze of the sun, just as there is between homelessness and sexual availability, and between the cultivation of intoxication and the social exclusion of its mediators. Wine always has more or less subversive connotations. The light of the sun is the light of the world through which the Beloved passes; in its eyes innocence is darkened.

The brothers are impelled by considerations of family honour, or else jealousy. The Beloved through her intrinsic seductiveness presents the potentiality of illicit love. Within the family, the play of desire and repression is especially perilous, and is complicated by competition for maternal affection: hence the paraphrase "my mother's sons." For the first time, the incest motif appears in the Song, albeit as a traumatised banishment of the forbidden sight.

At this point jealousy is experienced as outrage that the family refuses the shelter it should provide against a hostile world. Fraternal rivalry turns into complicity, to maintain a delicate balance of familial relations, based on the myth that infantile innocence = purity. The Dark Beloved is expelled from the family, as the source of defilement. Here other considerations arise, that will figure in subsequent episodes, namely family property and the sociology of gender.

To summarise the work so far: the antinomies of the dark beauty that account for its enigmatic character, since it suggests the possibility of integrating the unacceptable, are projected spatially onto the spectrum from desert to king, and historically in the growth of the Beloved, from an unburnt child in the midst of the family to a burnt dispossessed woman in the midst of society. The issues will be seen more clearly, in relief, as it were, if we turn to a passage (6:8–10) that is in all respects an inversion of ours. I will not discuss it in all its details, despite its fascinating richness, but merely concentrate on a few points of comparison.

שִׁשִּׁים הֵמָּה מְלָכוֹת וּשְׁמֹנִים
פִּילַגְשִׁים וַעֲלָמוֹת אֵין מִסְפָּר׃ אַחַת הִיא יוֹנָתִי תַמָּתִי
אַחַת הִיא לְאִמָּהּ בָּרָה הִיא לְיוֹלַדְתָּהּ רָאוּהָ בָנוֹת
וַיְאַשְּׁרוּהָ מְלָכוֹת וּפִילַגְשִׁים וַיְהַלְלוּהָ׃ מִי־זֹאת הַנִּשְׁקָפָה
כְּמוֹ־שָׁחַר יָפָה כַלְּבָנָה בָּרָה כַּחַמָּה אֲיֻמָּה כַּנִּדְגָּלוֹת׃

([6:8] There are sixty queens, and eighty concubines, and maidens without number.

[9] One is my dove, my pure one, one is she to her mother,
radiant to the one who gave her birth; the daughters saw her
and called her happy, the queens and concubines, and praised
her.
[10] Who is this who peers forth as the dawn, fair as the moon,
radiant as the sun, terrible as constellations?)

Here the dark Beloved is brilliant and pure (tammātî), adored at the
centre of society instead of being outcast from it. She is seen and praised
by the daughters, queens and concubines, instead of fearing their contempt and begging them not to look on her. She is radiant as the sun,
giving light to the world, the source of joyfulness. "The daughters saw
her and called her happy." Envy is strangely absent, though richly deserved.

There is one constant factor linking 1:5–6 and 6:8–10: hers is a natural beauty, as opposed to the cultural beauty of the queens and concubines. She is a dove, a wild creature of the rocks. The most remarkable
structural feature of the passage, however, is the fusion of two moments
at the furthest remove: the moment of birth with royal intimacy. This is
the ultimate image of integration: a "hieros gamos" of king representing
society with newborn baby. Opposed to it were all the forces of 1:5–6:
the brothers/the daughters/the sun. But here the brothers are absent; she
is her mother's unique child. The sun, instead of tormenting and dark-
ening her, has met its match: it is she who is "as radiant as the sun" and
gives light to the world; indeed the accumulation of celestial bodies, sun,
moon and stars, may imply her superiority.

There is consequently a progression from the innocence of birth to
adolescence; from the all-pervasive vital beauty to the cast out beauty,
repelled because it is too attractive. If the dark beauty in 1:6 tends the
fruit of Dionysus, the resplendent beauty of 6:9 is the source of ecstasy.
In a sense, she is the king's "baby," his protegée, and shares in his
licentious freedom and privilege. The luminous beauty, darkened in the
eyes of the world and the sun's glare, corresponds to the splendour of
the king, hidden behind curtains.

Let us pause for a moment to look at the images of the last verse:
"Who is this who peers forth as the dawn, fair as the moon, radiant as
the sun, terrible as constellations?" We have the emergence of day, the
coexistence of beauty and terror; but still more powerful is the combination of moon and sun, rulers of day and night, in her person. The
integration of dark and light takes the form of an ordered alternation in

Genesis and in common experience; the two luminaries introduce the calendar, days, months and seasons. At this point the Beloved transcends society and becomes a cosmic figure, immortal yet human, commensurate with the cycles of time and the immensity of space.

I have not the scope here for a full survey of the syntactic structure of 1:5–6, nor do I think it would contribute greatly to this particular argument. Nevertheless, one or two observations may be of interest.

The passage begins with a magnificent assertion of identity: "šehôrâ 'anî wenā'wâ (*I am* black and comely)." "This is what I am," it seems to say, "Good and bad, rustic, persecuted; take me or leave me." It ends with dispossession: "My own vineyard I have not kept." This forward movement in the surface of the text, fullness of self ◗ loss of self, is reversed in the syntactic structure: the main clauses are at the beginning of each sentence, and the subsequent units refer back to them. The similes in 1:5 "illustrate" the dark beauty; the sequence of events in 1:6 is subordinated to and explains her reluctance to be seen. In this case, syntax and logic correspond: the temporal sequence is from the end of the verse to its beginning. In both main clauses (I am black and comely . . . do not look on me) the Beloved is powerfully present; the symbolic context fills in her background and claims our sympathy. There is thus a movement from loss of self to fullness of self. Paradoxically, it is through being dispossessed, leaving her family and so on, that she finds herself; she becomes the keeper of vineyards, socially responsible, indignant, fascinatingly mysterious. In contrast, the well-mannered collectivity of daughters may seem colourless. Yet it is her individuality that courts degradation. Hence her proud annunciation is placatory, hoping to win an unassuming place in the world. This brings us to our opening enigma, that Beauty says, "Do not look on me!"

SECOND EPISODE: 8:11–12

כֶּרֶם הָיָה לִשְׁלֹמֹה בְּבַעַל הָמֹון נָתַן אֶת־הַכֶּרֶם לַנֹּטְרִים אִישׁ יָבִא
בְּפִרְיֹו אֶלֶף כָּסֶף: כַּרְמִי שֶׁלִּי לְפָנָי הָאֶלֶף לְךָ שְׁלֹמֹה וּמָאתַיִם
לְנֹטְרִים אֶת־פִּרְיֹו:

([8:11] Solomon had a vineyard in Baal-Hamon; he gave the vineyard to keepers; each one would bring for its fruit a thousand pieces of silver.

[12] My own vineyard is before me; yours, O Solomon, the thousand, and two hundred for the keepers of its fruit.)

This passage has especially intimate links with 1:5–6, because of their lexical and metaphorical correlations: the unique phrase "karmî šellî (my own vineyard)"; the occupation of "nōtēr/nōtērâ"; the play of *my* vineyard over against those of *others;* the figure of Solomon. It contrives to be even more enigmatic. In it, however, beauty undergoes a significant transformation.

The parable sets up a mystery: Whose is the vineyard? Are the vineyards in 8:11 and 8:12 one and the same? Is the vineyard—"karmî šellî"—the Beloved, as in 1:6, or is it something else?

Am I justified in calling it a parable, at least without indulging in a truism, since every action in poetry is metaphorical, simply by virtue of being in a poem? Unlike the other narratives in the Song, however, which are more or less pertinent to the affairs of lovers, the vicissitudes of Solomon's vineyard can only be understood as a similitude. The lease of one of Solomon's vineyards would hardly be immortalised in a love poem simply as a business record. In addition, it signals itself as parable through its setting in an indeterminate time, its semilegendary protagonist, its formulaic opening, and its apparent triviality. But if it is a parable, what does it illustrate?

In fact, the parable becomes enmeshed in paradox, belongs to what James Williams calls "the Wisdom of Counter-Order." The promise of narrative simplicity relaxes the reader, tempts and traps his anecdotal interest. In this way the parable is subversive.

It is also disturbing because it breaks its own rules. It begins like a ballad, a footnote to history. Yet in the next verse it becomes sharply personal. We do not know whether the first verse is set long ago, in the fabulous age of Solomon; it *was* his, "kerem hāyâ lišlōmōh," because he and it are no more; or whether he is alive and active, as the second verse suggests, and it has merely passed out of his possession. When the past tense is replaced by the present, Solomon is addressed directly, the first possibility is eliminated; we may imaginatively participate in that distant era, as the player enters the drama. The result is a foreshortening, a fusion of mythic time and real time, in which the present becomes fabulous. This in fact is one of the tricks of the parable: it entertains us at a distance with what apparently does not concern us, and then shows that we are involved, for example when David discovers that he is the subject of Nathan's parable.

The emblematic nature of the tale—its quality of fantasy, if you like—is intensified by the clearly allegorical overtones of the vineyard's location in the otherwise unknown Baal-Hamon, literally Lord/Baal of the multitude/wealth. The introductory formula: Vineyard + was + to So-and-So + in Allegorical Place Name is found also in Isaiah's Parable of the Vineyard, itself a love song (Isa. 5:1):

> kerem hāyâ lîdîdî beqeren ben šāmen
> (My beloved had a vineyard in Qeren-Ben-Shamen)

A variant occurs also in the Song, in 3:9:

> 'appiryôn 'āśā lô hammelek šelōmōh
> (Solomon made himself a palanquin)

In both these cases, likewise, the carefully distanced past vanishes: the vineyard is Israel, whom the Lord denounces; the daughters of Zion go out and gaze on Solomon (3:11).

The traditional introduction is a signal to the listener; he knows that he is listening to parable, to a form communicated through the singer. Through the ritualised formula, like "Once upon a time," the singer establishes his credentials, is invested with the authority of the autonomous, and therefore ever present, past. Parable, Northrop Frye tells us, is a subsidiary form of oracle.

Several critics attribute 8:11 or both verses to the Lover or poet, both of whom are identified with Solomon as one of their personae. There is no indication however of a change of speaker between 8:11 and 8:12, nor between 8:10 and 8:11; parsimony suggests that both 8:11 and 8:12, the exposition and development of the parable respectively, are part of her story. In the first verse her voice merges with that of the parable; in the second she projects herself and dramatises herself in its imaginary past. In 8:13 she is the singer, singing her own story. In other words, she is the observer and narrator of the events she experiences: the self splits into subject and object.

Solomon participates in the poem in two ways: as persona of the Lover and as sovereign. These generate the ambiguities of "kerem (the vineyard)," to which we now return.

Society cultivates intoxication in the vineyard; in the Song both it and its product wine have powerful erotic connotations. The vineyard at Baal-Hamon may well be the Beloved, the source of sexual intoxication, "the only one" (6:9). On the other hand, it may be his kingdom, the source of Dionysian luxury and power.

The name Baal-Hamon, Lord of Wealth or of the Multitude, draws attention to this second possibility: analogous to it are the allegorical place-names Heshbon and Bat-Rabbim in 7:5. But the toponym has another connotation, that of displaced local deities. Might there be a suggestion of fertility? Or of hubris?

If the vineyard is the Beloved, then one may suppose that 8:11 and 8:12 are contrasted: "Once upon a time," she says, "I was Solomon's vineyard; now I am my own." The difficulties start when one wonders what Solomon is doing giving her to "keepers," especially if the latter bring a thousand pieces of silver for her fruit. The third stich may mean that they *give* or *receive* the silver; or it may simply be an impersonal statement of value: *one would give.* Some critics have accordingly sought to identify the keepers with hired eunuchs, a clearly apologetic construction. The first possibility, that they give the silver, is both more daring and more realistic: Solomon has used her in political barter, instead of wearily consigning her to the harem. Although betrayal of their love is outrageous in the Song, in sober history it is merely sensible. Thus we encounter a profound opposition:

Way of the World $^+$ | Values of the Song $^-$
[$+$ = valued positively; $-$ = valued negatively]

If the vineyard is the kingdom, analogously those who tend its grapes are ministers, officials. He delegates responsibility in quest of the true, valuable vineyard, that of the Beloved. Consequently, the opposition is reversed:

Way of the World $^-$ | Values of the Song $^+$

In the eyes of the world, a hedonistic king who fails to care for his kingdom is unworthy of his throne: we may catch here a resonance of the traditional criticism of Solomon. But the painstaking work of the Song is to show that love is worth all pleasures and riches, for it alone is as strong as death.

A similar opposition between the ways of the world and the values of the Song has been found a few verses earlier in the sketch of the man who gives all the substance of his house for love and is accordingly despised.

"My own vineyard is before me," in 8:12, is an echo of "My own vineyard I did not keep" (lō' nātārtî) in 1:6. Now she is the keeper of her own vineyard, not those of the community; unlike Solomon, whose vineyard others maintain. Supposing this to be a declaration of independence, there is a disjunction between past and present, the vineyard that was Solomon's and is now hers. But if she is her own mistress, he equally has disengaged himself from her, handing her over to the "nōtrîm," in a mutual withdrawal. Self-possession is thus in the face of exploitation, and the consequence of rejection.

In 1:5–6 we noticed an underlying movement from loss of self to fullness of self, which is dynamically effected in the transformation from social outcast, who squanders her potential, to king's mistress and social luminary. Self-possession results from sexual consummation. The whole space of the poem separates "My vineyard is mine" from "My own vineyard I did not keep." If nothing else, the Song tells of the discovery of oneself through love. In a sense, this inversion of 1:6 in 8:12 encapsulates the total experience of reading the poem.

She may therefore be her own through being his, or having been his. Self-possession is a product of conjunction, instead of separation, as the daughters of Jerusalem would have it.

These contraries implicate the following clause "hā'elep lekâ šelō-mōh (Yours, O Solomon, the thousand)," which is likewise totally enigmatic. She may offer him "the thousand"; or tell him to keep the thousand he offers. The free gift from the fullness of herself complements the sense of pricelessness, that a woman who can be bought does not value herself, and is therefore valueless. The "thousand" either identifies her vineyard with Solomon's, or else establishes an equivalence; her vineyard is worth the kingdom, all he has to offer. If the thousand pieces of silver are the hireling's wages, she permits the king himself to be her retainer, when she says, "The thousand be yours, O Solomon." The two images, her vineyard and his, the Lover and the kingdom, represent a perpetual motion, whereby the king continually abandons his kingdom for the truly valuable Beloved, the source of fertility, only to use her in the service of the kingdom. Analogously, the Beloved preserves her vineyard so as to bestow it freely; through bestowing it she fosters it.

The questions we formulated at the beginning of this section—Whose are the vineyards? Are they the same? The Beloved or the kingdom?—cannot be truly answered, for each alternative is dependent on the other.

The last phrase, "And two hundred for the keepers of its fruit," is weird. I do not propose to guess at the significance of the opposition 200|1000. If the *keepers* are ministers (second alternative), or lovers (first alternative), they too are expected to participate in Solomon's joy or rejection. An analogous instance is 5:1, where *friends* and *lovers* are invited to feast in the Lover's garden. For love is socially dynamic; his intimacy gives pleasure to the king's entourage, as in 6:8–9, where the queens and concubines rejoice in the Beloved's light, even though the king enjoys her exclusively. On the other hand, if "the thousand be yours" is a rejection, then pointedly included in it is the whole hierarchy.

The enigma in this passage serves to present two quite different stories simultaneously, and to show their incompatible and inextricable coexistence. We have found therein two reversible oppositions: The way of the world/the values of the Song and conjunction/disjunction. The two may be superimposed: in a loveless world self-fulfilment is narrowly egotistic, coldly repressive; people are valued according to political status. The Pastoral opens the self to the other, sophistication to coarseness. In the poem, where metaphors unite the most discrete components, the play of conjunction and disjunction becomes exuberantly insistent.

In 1:5–6, the first pole was represented by the daughters of Jerusalem, the second by the Beloved. The oppositions of Dionysus and Apollo, integration and differentiation, that we found there clearly correspond to those we have just formulated, the poles of lascivious abandonment and worldly calculation.

There are, however, differences, both in structure and in substance. In 1:5–6 the sequence of events is clear: the beauty that does not wish to be seen, the burning and tormenting of the Beloved, and so on. The enigma is, as it were, intrinsic. Here it invades the superstructure, undermines the narrative. There we have the directness of speech, a present that invokes the past; here we have a faraway parable, a past that becomes present. The present is obscure, as the Beloved's plea is transparent. The voice of the parable, of traditional wisdom, is paradoxical, unintelligible. Its autonomous time invests the speaker with sanctity, with mystery. The Beloved, as the medium for that voice, makes its past her present, both as a comment on life in sequential time and as an affirmation of the timelessness in which love participates. We remember the ambivalent status of the oracle as the chthonic voice of Apollo, subversive of common sense and fixed truths, and yet the authenticating voice of a static society.

The movement from dispossession to fullness parallels a temporal shift: from the moment before to the moment after. In 1:5–6 the Beloved has not yet been admitted into society; in 8:11–12 the timeless erotic moment is juxtaposed with its passing. The parable looks back with wistful hindsight. The passage from before to after is that from innocence to experience, to a passé dignity from envied despised beauty.

Beauty now reappears, in disguise. For through all its perplexities the theme of the parable is plain: it is the metamorphosis of grapes into money, of love into a commodity. In time, the transience of ecstasy becomes social currency; for instance, sex is institutionalised as marriage. Silver, because it is imperishable, is a resource against disaster, a conservation of energy, accumulated through common sense, caution, foresight. Work is converted into silver, silver into pleasure; silver filters, and postpones the exuberance of pleasure. As a defensive reserve, it paradoxically betrays man's insecurity and impermanence. Therewith he manipulates his surroundings and controls the sources of pleasure, constructing his magnificent, defensive civilisation. Whereas in tending the vineyards, man participates in the process of nature, and enjoys the sweetness of the earth, through the Midas touch he makes process changeless; his greed becomes repressive, abstract. The transformation of Dionysiac intoxication is symbolised by a change of colour, from chthonic darkness to glittering whiteness.

For silver is beautiful, is a source of pleasure in itself. The beauty of silver is distant, indestructible. It has the purity of repression, and consequently is the root of corruption. For mastery of silver makes all pleasure available, postponed, imagined, and finally squandered. The agent of repression conceals in its splendour infinite wish fulfilment. Entirely similarly, the fairness of the daughters of Jerusalem is protected against their own desire.

Avaricious greed, miserly retention, conspicuous waste: the metaphorical language of money is derived from the nutritional cycle. Money is inedible, symbolic food. The anxious polarities of thrift and expenditure, manic extravagance and tight control, correspond to a phase of money as ex- crement. We thus witness the transformation of dark, fetid excrement into bright, incorruptible silver.

For silver is death in the service of life. If the dark Beloved represents the power of integration of life and death, the transformation into silver renders death immutable, tame, a changeless quantity.

A strange thing happens. The means of repression comes itself to stand for the thing repressed. Money becomes the agent of Dionysus, the instrument of social change, of life as process. And as is the way with such instruments, it enslaves its master. So man loves and is dominated by matter, as Marx's concept of alienation suggests. From being the means of obtaining pleasure, it becomes the compulsive pleasure itself.

Neurosis mistakes the surrogate for the source, symbolic food for real food. For reality is terrifying, mysterious, and ultimately deadly. The transactions of society, whereby love enters the poem, grapes the green-grocer's, ensures the diffusion of Dionysiac intensity. The single conjoined moment enters disjunctive time, inspiration becomes commonplace. The nuclear sentence in the passage is "hā'elep lekâ šelōmōh (Yours, O Solomon, the thousand)." All the others provide the setting; the last phrase is a tag or bobtail. "The thousand be yours, O Solomon," through its ambiguity, combines both poles in a harmonious relationship. It expresses self-validating pride, an assertion of identity worth all the silver in the world. But the pride comes out of receiving the homage of the world (Solomon, silver) and self-surrender, out of their fusion. The passage puts that which is beyond value in the marketplace; it is like the child's question "How much do you love me?" The random hyperbole, as well as being evidence for the metaphorical nature of the vineyard, clearly demonstrates the nonsense of equation. And yet sadly it happens: women become tokens, beauty is traded, wine merchants prosper.

In 6:9–10, the Beloved undergoes an apotheosis, from darkness to brilliance, a solar figure at the centre of society. As Marcia Falk points out, the word for "moon (lebānâ)," emphasises its whiteness. She is, as it were, living silver. The figures of the moon and the sun combine lunar periodicity with solar plenitude. Moreover, the last image in the sequence, "terrible as constellations," projects her wonder onto the patterns of fixed stars, in perpetual revolution. One thinks of Psalm 8:4: "If I look at the heavens, the work of your fingers, the moon and the stars that you have established," and its sense of the littleness of man. Now it is she who is equal to the cosmos. Astrology, which was known if not monotheistically sanctioned in Ancient Israel, is founded on an intuition of predestination, that everything is foreknown and therefore preexistent, and of a secret correspondence between things, by means of which our destiny is coded in the stars; now the stars are coded in her. She becomes a figure of Fate, the mystery of life and death, terrible and wondrous, accepted as pattern. Thus she integrates the forces that silver neutralises.

Third Episode: 8:8–10

אָחוֹת לָנוּ קְטַנָּה וְשָׁדַיִם אֵין לָהּ מַה־נַּעֲשֶׂה לַאֲחוֹתֵנוּ
בַּיּוֹם שֶׁיְּדֻבַּר־בָּהּ׃ אִם־חוֹמָה הִיא נִבְנֶה עָלֶיהָ טִירַת
כָּסֶף וְאִם־דֶּלֶת הִיא נָצוּר עָלֶיהָ לוּחַ אָרֶז׃ אֲנִי חוֹמָה
וְשָׁדַי כַּמִּגְדָּלוֹת אָז הָיִיתִי בְעֵינָיו כְּמוֹצְאֵת שָׁלוֹם׃

([8:8] We have a little sister, and she has no breasts. What shall we do for our sister on the day when she shall be spoken for?

[9] If she is a wall, we will build on her a turret of silver; and
if she is a door we will enclose her with boards of cedar.
[10] I am a wall and my breasts are like towers; therefore I
was in his eyes as one who found peace.)

This passage immediately precedes 8:11–12, and so it might seem
odd to discuss it after it; this is because 8:11–12 exhibits closer lexical
correspondences with 1:5–6: "karmî šellî" and so on. Chapter 8,
verses 8–10 uses different materials, yet it combines the image of silver
from 8:11–12 with the theme of familial relationships in 1:5–6 and 6:8–
10. Its relationship with 1:5–6, the starting point of our discussion, is
one of antithesis, as will appear; yet it offers the possibility of harmon-
ising the disjunctions that until now have been our principal concern.

The first ambiguity concerns the speaker, who could be the brothers
of 1:5–6, sisters, or the Beloved herself. I consider it to be the latter, since
the other views would involve introducing new characters without textual
authority, a bad critical procedure. Moreover, it necessitates supposing a
"flashback" or poor eyesight to account for the discrepancy between the
nonexistence of breasts, as seen by the "brothers," and their full development, as declared by the Beloved. This precipitates the invention of
stories, romances woven round the text. My view is simply that the
Beloved speaks, as a member of her family, about her little sister, who is
growing up.

In 8:8–10 the enigma is overt, instead of appearing through a paradoxical action, as in 1:5–6, or an ambiguous metaphor, in 8:11–12. It is
an unanswered question: "What shall we do on the day she shall be
spoken for?"

The text contemplates two hypothetical futures: that she be a wall
and that she be a door. If the metaphors had a clear, culturally defined
meaning, it has been lost. Once again we meet our ambiguous "wĕ":
"If she is a wall . . . and / but if she is a door." They are thus either
adversative and/or complementary.

That there is some opposition is evident from 8:10, in which the
assertion "I am a wall" explains the Beloved's success. What remains
unclear, however, is whether "wall" and "door" are two kinds of beauty
or character, both of which are of value, or whether they are contrasted.
In the latter case, if the wall wins the Lover's favour and is crowned with
silver, the door would correspondingly be unattractive.

The older critics saw in this a straightforward opposition of virtue:
the wall is an unassailable woman, the door is open to all comers.

Tur-Sinai, followed by Gordis and others, remark that "wall" and "door" are traditional synthetic parallelisms; like the wall, the door is normally barred, and consequently they believe that both are expressive of a chaste reserve.

This ambiguity is compounded by that of *nāṣûr* in the last stich. It may mean to "enclose," but also to "adorn," "fashion," or "besiege." Taking only the first view, the older critics found here confirmation of the brothers' cruelty (and their own attribution), in a diabolical punishment for the girl's imprudence, namely, seclusion in a cedar cubbyhole; Krinetzki puts forward essentially the same interpretation in a milder form: if the brothers feel that she is a bit too vivacious, they will sedulously protect her. If, however, *nāṣur* means "we will adorn" or "fashion," it parallels *nibneh* (we will build) in the first stich, and the two images are complementary.

The parallel superstructures, the turret of silver and the boards of cedar, have a dual function, as fortifications and embellishments. Accordingly, both "wall" and "door" are ambiguous, as only Albert Cook has perceived. The turret is seen and glitters from afar; the planks are carved from costly wood. The Beloved is an attractive fortress; attractive and barred presumably because she is worth defending. However, if the wall tipped with silver and the door barricaded with cedar share the qualities of being rich and formidable, they are also antithetical.

Silver is conspicuous, the parapet catches the eye; analogously, the Tower of David in 4:4 glitters with the thousand shields of the warriors, that both repel attack and are a splendid ornament. Cedar, however, is strong and dark, associated, as we have seen, with smell and masculinity. The materials are appropriate to their tasks; for in a defensive network walls are visible, doors are concealed.

If the door raises the question of chastity, clearly it corresponds to the vagina; like the vagina, the door may be open or closed. If, in 8:10, the relationship of the breasts to the person is that of the tower to the wall, the tenor of the latter is equally transparent: it is the body, in which the "I" is contained. The body is conspicuous, the vagina is secret. The one attracts aesthetically, at a distance; the other communicates chemically, unconsciously, especially through smell, whose pervasiveness annuls differences.

At puberty, "the day when she shall be spoken for," the body expresses itself by developing breasts, the vagina through the growth of pubic hair, to which the planks of cedar may be compared, as the towers are compared to breasts. Both are powerfully erogenous, the pubic hair through concealing the genitalia, the breasts through announcing their presence. Therein may be discerned the relationship between them: the breasts, like the face, make sexuality aesthetic; they refer metonymically to the reticent vagina, that in them expresses itself socially, discreetly. The pubic hair, by screening the vulva, makes it mysterious, inexpressible; and hence initiates the process of linguistic diffusion. If the body represents a sexual potential, common to both man and woman, the vagina is the essence of femininity. At puberty, the emergence of breasts feminises the body, while the pubic hair disguises the vagina.

If in 1:5–6 Beauty comes from outside civilisation, here it is enshrined in its centre; it is, as it were, a city under siege. The wall and the door are complementary and antithetical, activating opposite poles of the aesthetic experience. The wall contains the door, without which it could not be entered; if in this case, the wall divides self and other, the door provides the means of communication, either open or closed. The wall differentiates, the door unites, like the body and the vagina, that stand for Apollo and Dionysus respectively. The one is transmitted to the conscious eye, that appraises objectively, the other to the sensitive nose, in whose reactions disgust and ecstasy are inextricably mingled.

No woman, of course, is all vagina or all figure; the schematic metaphors isolate qualities that are always mingled in real life, that manifest themselves with different emphases. Wall and door are different types of attractiveness that yet have a complementary relationship. It is with pride that the Beloved asserts that she is a wall and not a door, and that therefore she met with the Lover's approval. For the wall is bold and manifest; on the other hand, the door is secret. The relationship between wall and door is that between body and genitalia, the one articulating the other.

If the theme of 8:11–12 is the transformation of grapes into money, here it is the process of ripening. In her little sister the Beloved recognises herself, and her own progress from childhood through puberty. The little sister is an image of herself, in the sequence of generations; in this sense she is "a flashback," as Lys says. Instead of incestuous jealousy and expulsion from the family, puberty here leads to identification.

The child is irresponsible, like Solomon or the Bedouin in 1:5; like the dark Beloved, she comes from outside society and has to be initiated into it. Before she has breasts no one talks about the little sister; it is not yet the day when, literally, "it shall be spoken about her." Puberty makes her a point of general interest, the subject of gossip and intrigue. For especially the adolescent presents the question: "Whose shall she be?" It is quite possible that "bayyôm šeyyedubbar bāh" (the day when she shall be spoken for)" idiomatically alludes to marriage negotiations, though the evidence is slender; its range of reference is far wider, however, embracing every gossipy context in which her name might be mentioned. For behind this question there is another, more pervasive one—namely, "What shall she be?"—which one asks of a child more as an expression of wonder and an excuse for fantasy than for a sober answer. If the vagina/door is an unanswered question—is it open or closed?—the plain wall signifies the absence of questioning, that she has not yet become the subject of speculation. Only when mediation occurs, when the body is sexualised and the vagina concealed, do the questions become active, tangible.

The little sister does not answer these questions, and in fact does not talk at all. She is completely passive, the subject matter of discourse, not the speaker. No doubt there is a sociological reference here. The question of sexual choice is formulated by time and by others, by *the day* on which *it shall be spoken* about her. The family adorn and manipulate her, with turrets of silver and planks of cedar. They participate even in her physical development, an idea that is less bizarre than it first seems if one considers the elaborate beautification of nubile daughters in many cultures. Her body is appropriated by the family, as a social asset. The identification of the Beloved with the little sister as an image of herself leads to her transformation into an image of herself, the image the family imposes on her. She is almost literally gilded, to become social currency, decked with silver and cedar.

The little sister corresponds to the fair daughters of Jerusalem: light-coloured, sheltered, dependent. In her, the Beloved contemplates an adolescence in which the family acts as a bridge between the child and the public world, which becomes, as it were, its extension, entered through peaceful transition, instead of abrupt violence. The little sister is then an "altera ego," in whom she recognises not her own past—for there is no single story in the Song—but a different one.

The images of 8:9 foreshadow the uncertainties of the future; there is no knowing what the little sister will be. Whereas the Beloved appears to control the little sister, to dress her like a doll, in reality all she can do is respond to the child's unfolding disposition. Nothing more can be said about the child's future; she turns to her own past, perhaps as an example of a successful journey, possibly for assurance against those limitless perspectives. The "altera ego" now becomes herself: she presents herself as a wall with towers. The contrast little sister/dark Beloved reverses itself:

she is a wall and not a door, chaste—if that is a connotation of wall—well-formed, defended. The dispossessed woman is now self-possessed, that is, possessed by the family. Yet therewith she attains a forthright independence: the breasts are like towers, dominant, assertive. As in 1:5, she thrusts herself forward, with the first-person pronoun: *I am* ('anî) a wall, just as previously she had said, "I am ('anî) black and comely." Yet she fulfils herself in the eyes of the other: "Therefore I was in his eyes as one who found peace." "Kemôse'ēt šālôm" can have three meanings, the first two of which are antithetical and complementary:

1. to find peace
2. to bring peace
3. to surrender, of a city

Peace is the completion of the process, a perfect integration of self and other. Dionysiac intensity ends in tranquillity, when the desire becomes fulfilment. For the desire is for tranquillity, the absence of desire, in a stable and blissful harmony. Dionysus wishes his own negation or catharsis, in which Apollo, the serene, differentiating principle, is likewise integrated. "In his eyes" may be a synecdoche for himself: her individuality is fostered for his good opinion. But it may also mean literally his eyes, because they are beautiful; by gazing at his eyes she finds peace. For eyes have a dual function, corresponding to the differentiating and de-differentiating principles. They are observers, through which we become aware of the objective world, in all its manifold difference; yet in them man feels he gets behind appearances, that the subjective personality becomes manifest. The exchange of eyes, like sexual intercourse, annuls differences, communicates without words, "where we cannot speak," where words are unnecessary, obstructive, or deceptive. The beauty of eyes is especially interesting, for they can only unite without touching, at a psychic distance; their objective separateness is the condition for their fusion. "In his eyes" she finds peace, because there objectively—through vision—she is absorbed in the other. Yet likewise she gives peace, for his eyes are filled with her presence. She looks at his eyes that look at her/hers; in him she finds a reflection of herself, of their mutual reciprocity. This is also an image of surrender—the third ambiguity of "môse'ēt šālôm"; the city is fortified, the girl is trained for this moment, when culture gives way to nature. The Beloved, through her upbringing, preserves the child through the family into the adult world; innocence survives in the guise of purity. She remains a combination of dark and light, in which the darkness is expressed through the light, as the eyes reveal the mysterious person.

The city surrenders to the Lover, of whose persona as king we have had several illustrations. If in 1:5 he is hidden behind curtains, and in 8:11–12 has to choose between vineyards, here the curtains/wall are the city, and the fusion of love becomes an image of political harmony. In 1:5, the king is both the centre of society and inaccessible to it, as the source of Dionysiac energy. Here he enters the kingdom from outside, and the city relinquishes its defences. The positions are thus reversed: in 1:5 the king personifies the city, and the Beloved is the rural outsider; here the Beloved is the city, and the king the stranger.

There has been a fourth suggested meaning for "kemôṣe'ēt šālôm": that it is the emergence or sparkling of the Evening Star, Shalem. If so, she is the intermediary between night and day, as in 6:10. There is a complementary link between the two passages, as Dahood and Schoville point out: Shalem in our verse is matched by "šāḥar (the dawn star/the dawn)" in 6:10. She is the messenger of the tense serenity of twilight, the cosmic conflict and harmonious alternation of light and dark. On this interpretation, "in his eyes" may simply mean "to him"; but if taken literally, his eyes would become a metaphor for the sky in which she shines, a brilliant divine point in his immensity. The moment of consummation then reconciles two extremes: plenitude with particularity. This recalls the opening paradox that lovers can be distinctly aware of each other and yet merged with each other. It revives the oceanic feeling of earliest infancy: the emergence of consciousness from infinite space.

The little sister, like the daughters of Jerusalem, is cultivated in the midst of society; her beauty is the result of careful nurture. It is the beauty of civilisation, as opposed to the wild, subversive beauty of the Beloved in 1:5. If in 1:5–6, the Beloved is a threat, and in 6:8–10 is adopted and adored, here the threat is disguised, innocence is preserved through change, and once again the Beloved presents the promise of fulfilment. The ways of the world thus subtly confirm the values of the Song; the citadel is elaborated so as to be abandoned in love. There is continuity between infancy, puberty, and sexual consummation; an untroubled adolescence whose cost is self-effacement.

Beautifying hides and heightens sexual attraction; postponing it at a distance. Yet it may be enjoyed, by the girl as well, as fantasy. She is turned into an artistic whimsical ornament, seductive and elusive. On the level of language, this is the work of the Song; on that of nature, it may be any object that catches the fancy, the world as metalanguage used by the lovers. The transformation of love into silver that we have discovered is here mediated; love becomes art, and is therefore preserved for its time and for ever. But there is also sadness: that women become marital objects, that they are fussed over and grow to be something "in his eyes," according to one of its ambiguous meanings.

The enigma here is that of the future—the realm of fantasy "par excellence"—and it is expounded through a parody of legal formulae. Law dreams of controlling the future; it regulates the appropriate response to circumstances, in clear and definite language. Here it classifies the future under two categories, which might be equivalent or opposed; moreover, as we have seen, the second apodosis is utterly inconclusive. The expectation of a clear directive is thus confounded; whereas law deals with practical reality, the language here is metaphorical. If a metaphor signifies a person, in law abstractions replace the individual. There is, however, another perspective, that is both a perception and a criticism. Our verse cannot be taken seriously as law, with its stereotyped formula "If so-and-so . . . then such-and-such," because of its sheer incommensurability. How does one set about building a silver parapet on a person, or declare her "wall" or "door"? The point is not so much that these are metaphorical, but that the law itself has a poetic function. In particular, as the medium of repression, it paradoxically activates some of society's darkest sadistic impulses. The family's behaviour towards the little sister, whether it locks her up, fashions her, or festoons her, expresses through the ambiguity of the verbs the ambivalence of its relations. As in 1:6, a wicked little sister is a challenge, to be coped with through a mingling of aggression and affection. And from all the energy that is devoted to constructing her in the family's image, she emerges: "I am. . . ."

Syntactically, the passage is a progression from negation to affirmation, from passive to active. The opening verse couples a qualified, minimised subject—"We have a little sister"—with a negation—"And she has no breasts"; this is followed by a clause expressive of the absence of action and bewilderment—"What on earth shall we do for our sister?" In a doubly subordinated position, as a relative clause enclosed in a prepositional phrase, is the most powerful verb in the sentence [8d] "bayyôm šeyyedubbar bāh (on the day when she shall *be spoken* for)." But it is in the passive mood: it is action done impersonally *to* the little sister, the opposite of action done by her.

Thus we have four units:

8a	'āḥôt lānû qetannâ	Diminished Noun Phrase
	we have a *little* sister	$(+NP)$
8b	wešādayim 'ēn lāh	Negation $(-NP)$
	she has no breasts	
8c	mah na'aśeh la'aḥōtēnû	Absence of action, questioning
	what shall we do for	
	our sister	$(-VP)$
8d	bayyôm šeyyedubbar bāh	Passive $(-VP)$
	on the day when she shall	
	be spoken for?	

Moreover, 8b is coupled with 8d: the day when she shall be spoken for is the day when she has breasts. The transformation from $^-$NP—$^+$NP, from being without to being with breasts, leaves her exposed to attention, to being the recipient of action, and results in passivity. Now if we combine 8a and 8c, we have the following sentence: "What shall we do for our little sister?" The sister is thus the passive object of both action and speech.

Chapter 8, verse 9, alternates a nominal phrase with a verbal phrase, combining wonder with busy activity. We now know what they will do, but the little sister is still passive. The negation of 8c becomes positive, while the passivity of 8d is unchanged. What is most distinct about the verse, however, is its careful symmetry. The formulae are identical in every particular, even to the two-word construct that is the object of each action:

9b	nibneh 'ālêhâ *ṭîrat kāsep*	VP(VP + [PP] + NP)
9d	nāṣûr 'ālêhâ *lûaḥ'ārez*	VP(VP + [PP] + NP)

> (We will build on her a turret of silver;
> We will enclose her with boards of cedar)

and on which each concludes. As we know, in content they combine complementarity with antithesis, to produce an ideal synthesis. The clauses are constructed as artfully as the city; they are in themselves evidence for the playful, inventive character of their alternative futures. Dependent on "What shall we do?" bewilderment turns here to fantasy.

In 8:10 the subject emerges from this complex of questions and conditional clauses; it asserts itself very plainly and boldly:

10a 'anî ḥômâ
10b wešāday kammigdālôt

(I am a wall
And my breasts are like towers.)

We find here an echo of the beginning of verse 8: "We have a little sister and she has no breasts." Both combine two Noun Phrases. But here the negatives have turned positive, and the subject speaks. In time, and as a consequence ('az), she transfers herself to the other:

10c 'az hāyîtî be'ênāyw
10d kemōṣe'ēt šālôm

(Therefore I was in his eyes
As one who found peace.)

These are both Noun Phrases and Verb Phrases, and strongly affirmative. In 10c the verb "hāyîtî (I was)" is both action and copula; in 10d, "kemōṣe'ēt," as participle, is both verb and noun. Moreover, both protagonists are the subjects, or rather they are the shared subject: "I was . . . in his eyes," as they are through the various ambiguities, the permutations of giving and receiving, in "kemōṣe'ēt šālôm." Finally, 10b and 10d are linked through their similes, underlined by alliteration: "KaMMigdālôt . . . KeMōṣe'ēt šālôm": like towers that give and receive peace.

The movement from negation to affirmation, from absence of self to fullness of self, coupled with the cyclic recurrence of 8ab in 10ab, and the integration of syntactic components in 10cd, corresponds, as we have seen, to the thematic patterning of the passage. In 1:5–6 we found a syntactic current from loss of self to fullness of self runs counter to the surface movement from fullness of self to loss of self. As in other respects, 8:8–10 is in opposition to 1:5–6; syntax and content are in concord, as the girl with the city.

	Subject	Attributes	Verb	Address	Mode
8	Little Sister	no breasts	no action	no speech	Passive, Object
9a	Wall		build		Active, Object
9b	Door		enclose		Active, Object
10	I	+ wall + breasts		speech	Active + Passive Verb + Noun

Fourth Episode: 1:7–8

הַגִּידָה לִּי שֶׁאָהֲבָה֙ נַפְשִׁ֔י אֵיכָ֣ה תִרְעֶ֔ה אֵיכָ֖ה תַּרְבִּ֣יץ
בַּֽצָּהֳרָ֑יִם שַׁלָּמָ֤ה אֶֽהְיֶה֙ כְּעֹ֣טְיָ֔ה עַ֖ל עֶדְרֵ֥י חֲבֵרֶֽיךָ׃ אִם־לֹ֧א
תֵדְעִי֙ לָ֔ךְ הַיָּפָ֖ה בַּנָּשִׁ֑ים צְֽאִי־לָ֞ךְ בְּעִקְבֵ֣י הַצֹּ֗אן וּרְעִי֙ אֶת־
גְּדִיֹּתַ֔יִךְ עַ֖ל מִשְׁכְּנ֥וֹת הָרֹעִֽים׃

([1:7] "Tell me, you whom my soul loves, where do you graze,
where do you rest your sheep at noon, for why should I be
like a wanderer by the flocks of your friends?"
[8] "If you know not, fairest among women, go forth in the
sheep tracks, and pasture your kids by the shepherds' huts.")

Chapter 1, verses 7–8, corresponds to 1:5–6 as 8:8–10 does to 8:11–
12, both syntagmatically and through its recombination of materials.
Like them, its meaning is extremely elusive; yet in it we return to our
starting-point, to the place of beauty in the world, the heat of the sun,
and the motif of shame. Rhetorically, however, it is a development on
8:8–10, in that an overt question meets a paradoxical answer. Whereas in
8:8–10 the question "What will she be?" is unanswerable, here the reply
makes the enigma more perplexing.

In her Lover's presence, the Beloved is preoccupied with his absence.
She tries to fix the next rendezvous, which is the result of separation: the
two lovers have different paths in the world. A whole morning has to be
endured. Furthermore, even in the present she lacks assurance that he is
really there, that he is really listening. Almost all of the first half of her
sentence is taken up with conative expressions, whose principal function
is to elicit attention. This indeed is the sole function of "haggîdâ lî (Tell
me)" followed by the vocative, "you whom my soul loves"; the epithet
combines flattery with an inkling of the urgency of the message and the
responsibility of the recipient to listen kindly. The alliterative doubling
of "êkâ tir'eh 'êkâ tarbîṣ baṣṣāhorāy îm (Where do you graze, where do
you rest your sheep at noon?)" intensifies the question; the repetition
implies anxiety that the question would not be heard the first time, not
taken seriously. Another fear is that the Lover is reluctant to answer and
hence needs pressing, a suggestion prompted by the second hemistich.
For there the Beloved complains of her neglect, and demands to know
the reason for her still hypothetical ill-treatment. In this way the indirect
accusation of indifference is combined with one of undeserved callous-

ness, so as perhaps to ensure a comforting answer, such as righteous protestation.

The lover's reply begins with a strange conditional: "If you know not, fairest among women. . . ." If she knew, she would have no need of asking. To all appearances, the clause is redundant. Perhaps he insinuates that she should know, and therefore her winning artful question is merely conversational; he proceeds to match her, both in the symmetrical artifice of his utterance, and in its euphuistic ambiguity. For by the end of the verse we still do not know whether he has revealed his whereabouts. "Go forth in the sheep tracks," for instance, sounds like the advice of a good detective, but we have no means of telling whether it is his sheep she should follow, nor whether she was adept at distinguishing his sheep tracks from those of any other. But the crucial ambiguity is "by the shepherds' huts." Is this phrase synonymous with "by the flocks of your friends"? If so, will he be there, among his friends? The combination of these alternatives produces the following possibilities:

A. If "by the huts" is not "by the flocks" and the shepherds graze far afield, then it seems likely that he is arranging an intimate colloquy.
B. If "by the huts" *is* "by the flocks":
   (a) He is with them, a shepherd among shepherds, and invites the Beloved to join their amicable company.
or (b) He is not there, and leaves "the fairest among women" to be a *wanderer* ('ōteyâ), as she feared in the first verse.

The guessing game—Does she know? Does he tell?—leaves the question of their meeting again open, indeed for the rest of the poem. The alternatives comprise two realities: the uncertain divisive future and the assurance of love. She may know where he will be, simply because he always has his lunch on the same spot, and their meetings are recurrent; or it may be intuitive knowledge, as Albert Cook suggests, citing the emphatic "ethic dative" "lāk ([lit.] if you do not know *for yourself*)." This is compatible with ignorance; for intuition is a connectedness between parties, whatever their physical separation. In a sense, it is a statement of simultaneous presence and absence. The dialogue, however, reveals their lurking absence, even when physically present. The ambiguities preserve a necessary distance, enabling them to be in touch without finally meeting. In this way absence even when present is in apposition with presence when absent, and the moment of contact is diffused through subsequent adventures, through memory, through intuition. Absence when present and presence when absent mediate between conjunction and disjunction.

This process takes the lovers into society, where they meet or are separated, an enigma communicated, as we have seen, through the alternative meanings of "by the shepherds' huts." Joviality (Ba) is a middle term between separation by society (Bb) and intimacy within society (A). The Conjunction (A) implies an opposition between *shepherds' huts* and *friends' flocks* (i.e., lovers/society) which are in fact paired, since the shepherds return to their huts each night. The lovers are alone, at the site of sleep, the pastoral centre at the point of departure for the shepherds' wanderings, and hence for the question "Where will you be?" This corresponds to the possibility of meeting, intuitively, while apart, of simultaneous presence and absence. The lovers are at the centre of a society that is apparently unaware of them.

The mediant possibility, that they meet in company, requires a dissimulation, wherewith their love is acknowledged, but constrained; possibly recognised and welcomed by society, but not too openly. This coexistence corresponds to the absence when present of the dialogue, to conversational allusiveness.

The third possibility (Bb) requires more examination, especially of the Beloved's complaint "For why should I be like an "ōṭeyâ' by the flocks of your friends?" The word 'ōṭeyâ is obscure, and has been variously interpreted: as a "wanderer," a "prostitute," a woman "veiled" in mourning or with darkened sight, or even "one picking lice." Beauty is grief-stricken, astray, for sale, disconsolate or bored, because of her Lover's absence. Here society is the scene of repression, where lascivious women attract shame, as in 1:5–6, and are sexually exploited. The Beloved's complaint is voiced as a question: "Why should I be like a wanderer?" She is on the fringe of masculine society, to which the Lover belongs, as a "friend." If he dismisses her, he makes her into a victim of the mockery to which spurned sexual partners are subject. He becomes a collaborator with his "friends," since it is his refusal to tell that is the occasion for her desperate search and exposes her to abuse. On the one hand, he is an adoring lover; on the other, a member of the fraternity that despises women. Her knowledge is of the love that survives despite conformity; and her grief is that this love is not found among "friends," that it is separate.

The three possibilities are variants of the same opposition that we found in 8:11–12: the ways of the world and the values of the Song. In the eyes of the Song and the Lover she is "the fairest among women," the head of the female hierarchy, unique and splendid in 6:9; but as a "friend," he turns her into an "'ōṭeyâ," a vagabond, prostitute, and so on, dispossessed and hence valueless. The three stories can be collated accordingly:

A. The values of love at the unconscious heart of society.
Ba. Love becomes socialised . . . Love ◆ way of the world.
Bb. Love rejected by society . . . Way of the world ◆◀ values of the Song.
  [◆◀ = opposed to; ◆ = congruent with]

There is in truth no answer to the Beloved's protest, and I would agree with Phyllis Trible in seeing this as an essential part of the subversive message of the Song. In this episode, however, the transformation becomes a means of integrating the Beloved into society, of reconciling received attitudes with anarchic desire. If, in 8:11–12, intoxication turns into silver, and in 8:8–10, beauty becomes art, here the Beloved is a shepherdess. She is an economic asset, contributing to the wealth of the community, and in this way parallel to the keeper of vineyards in 1:6. But the terms are now inverted. To begin with, the Beloved cares for her own kids, which are a sign of her status, not those of others. Whereas she is made into a keeper of vineyards through disapprobation, she now becomes a shepherdess among shepherds, a comrade of those whose illtreatment she feared. If the shepherds are paradigmatically related to the brothers, as male collectivities who torment the Beloved, she now returns to the family, one might say to the fold. The sexes are equal in their employment, in their social roles, whereas in 1:6 the Beloved was driven out because she was forward, that is, acted sexually as a male.

It is because she "knows" the value of the Lover that the Beloved searches for him and risks humiliation, assuming the guises of the "'ōṭeyâ"; her confusion, "not knowing," is a function of true knowledge. The shepherdess follows the same path, but has a place in society, where she *might* find the Lover. The lovers are parted by the day and its tasks, society and time, and it is there that the Beloved envisages their meeting, at noon, while grazing. The heat of the sun reverses its emotive value: that which darkens the complexion is now the ally of love. Its fierceness causes them to seek shelter, and is conducive to drowsiness and amorous suggestion, while the flocks graze together, an image of their langorous discourse. If the day is associated with conscious differentiation, and sunlight with the objectivity of vision, the centre of the day and the excess of sunlight bring about a reversion to unfocussed half-consciousness, parallel to the relationship (A) between the friends' flocks and the shepherds' huts, which the lovers visit at noon when the occupants are away, but which are the centre of their activities. The siesta in the middle of the day is parallel to intimacy at the heart of society.

Diurnal love thus corresponds to a flooding of consciousness, and reproduces the transformation between solar darkness and brilliance, which we discerned in 6:8–10.

However, the fundamental difference between the two occupations, the keeper of vineyards and the shepherdess, is that between them intoxication becomes continuance. The dark Beloved tends the fruit of Dionysus, which we connected with her sexual hoard, while the shepherdess takes care of the sources of wool, milk and meat, society's clothing and nourishment. Animal lascivious energy is tamed and put to use, while in the vineyards and vats society turns natural sweetness into Dionysiac subversion.

Whereas in 1:5 the Beloved's is a tale of exploitation in a stratified community, and exemplifies the interaction of city and country through conformity and violence, the commonwealth of shepherds is egalitarian, and associated in the Pastoral with sweet amours, tolerance, and sympathy with nature. The earth gives freely, as in the Golden Age; the shepherds are its untroubled and paternalistic masters. In contrast, the agriculturalist toils for its harvest; he is the base of civilisation, while the shepherd stands somewhat outside it.

It would be inappropriate to dwell on the image of the shepherd in the Pastoral, since apart from this passage it hardly occurs in the Song of Songs. The shepherd is characterised by an intimacy with wildness. His flocks graze on the hills; he is sustained by and knowledgeable of the rough terrain. He is an image of harmony, of nature beneficent to man, and man at ease with and respectful of nature. He is a master of tranquillity and of song, of a natural simple order. It is for this reason that the work is so enviable, as an agent of integration, as well as because of its lazy recurrence that promotes a sense of timelessness.

The Beloved as "'ōṭeyâ" disturbs this serenity, as well as our idealisation of pastoral virtue. She is only *like* an "'ōṭeyâ," however; in reality, she is a shepherdess, and the most beautiful of women. The three terms, "'ōṭeyâ," shepherdess, and fairest of women, form a continuum, uniting extremes of beauty and ugliness, envy and contempt, which in 1:5–6 are represented by the Dark Beloved. The "'ōṭeyâ" is wildness in action, the Dionysiac spirit that haunts the fringes of the Pastoral. "The fairest among women" is reminiscent of 6:8–10, and the splendour of the court; the phrase is associated with the daughters of Jerusalem, who employ it in 5:9 and 6:1. Through her beauty she represents the city (Jerusalem and Tirzah in 6:4), man's achievement when liberated from subsistence. Thus they stand for wildness and civilisation respectively, Dionysus and Apollo, licentious subversion and sophistication; in other words, all the tensions underlying the Pastoral. Yet the Beloved is also a shepherdess— a middle term, like the daughters of Jerusalem—whose kids are in complementary antithesis with the Lover's sheep. Between the contrary pressures of the striving for civilised perfection and the craving for a return to original innocence is a simple conservatism, motivated by neither ambition nor regression.

The Lover's compliment "hayyāpâ bannāšîm (fairest among women)" contrasts with "še'āhabâ napšî (whom my soul loves)," with which the Beloved addresses him. "Fairest among women" is a gesture of objective appreciation that perceives her relative to others, no matter with what superiority. It contributes to the enigmatic quality of the Lover's speech, that sets her at a distance, both desirable and detached. "Whom my soul loves" defines their relationship, without regard to others; whereas beauty refers to appearance, "whom" implies that she loves him for himself, with her "soul," not her looks. She speaks objectively of her "nepeš," as if love were something that happened through her, that forces her to become an "'ōṭeyâ," a victim of shame. Unconscious Dionysiac possession thus meets objective, if flattering, appraisal, to produce the quandaries of knowing and not knowing, simultaneous presence and absence, that pervade the dialogue.

If the dialogue measures the distance between the lovers, revealing fear, rage and evasiveness in its sweet phrases, the lovers hear each other's voices. If they are present, and not absent to each other—concerned about the future—this is the sole content of the dialogue: the voice that speaks it. It is surprising how much of lovers' talk consists precisely of this: voice, that speaks beyond the differentiations of language. The superfluity of language in the lovers' discourse—"Tell me," "If you know not," with its redundant "lāk" and so on—has, on the one hand, a conative function, that activates attention; less obtrusively, it transfers it from the thoroughly obscure message to the sound, from tenor to vehicle. The seductiveness of the voice is aided by the mellifluousness of the language; communication becomes play. In the Beloved's speech, we have, for instance, the alliterative parallelism already cited: "'êkâ tir'eh 'êkâ tarbîṣ baṣṣāhorāyîm ('ēkâ tr 'ēkâ trbṣ bṣr)"; in the Lover's reply there is the rhyme of "'im lō'TEDe'I LAK . . . Ṣe'I LAK be'iqebê haṣṣō'n U-Re'I" . . . (If *you know* not . . . *go forth* in the sheep tracks, and *graze* . . .)."

The repartee has in fact the character of a duet, with its symmetrical construction and counterpoint of meanings. As in a duet, the voices intertwine, merge and separate. Moreover, the voices couple with that of the poet, to fashion the poem.

In the classical Pastoral, the shepherd is a metaphor for the poet, whose songs he sings. It is a return to an archaic language, in which sound, meaning, and sensory experience are only just differentiating, a return to a pasture where the poet writes in time to the eternal recurrence of the words, in a tranquil intoxication, uniting the twin poles of the Dionysiac encounter. Poetry is a listening, to the earth, to things, controlled and critical. William Berg introduces his illuminating discussion of the Pastoral with the following quotation:

> Often I am permitted to return to a meadow . . .
> an eternal pasture folded in all thought.

POSTSCRIPT: 1:9, 1:15–16

Beauty in the Song is communicated principally by metaphor, a complex system of alliance between the inexpressible self and the definable universe. The work of comparison obscures the reality of the person by clothing her in images. In this way, it contributes to the aesthetic process that distances the object of desire. The images are intricate compounds of objective sensory and emotional correlations and deeply disturbing symbolism. We find a good example in the verse immediately following the passage we have just discussed:

לְסֻסָתִי֙ בְּרִכְבֵ֣י פַרְעֹ֔ה דִּמִּיתִ֖יךְ רַעְיָתִֽי׃

([1:9] To a mare in Pharaoh's chariots I have compared you, my love.)

A horse in fine fettle is an exhilaratingly beautiful animal, especially when richly caparisoned; in other words, when it is metonymically identified with its owner, and shares in his value. A good example is the aesthetic function of the horse in the equestrian statue. The horse and its rider form a unit, especially in warfare, in the heroic code of chivalry. The horse combines the two tendencies that have been the subject for our discussion: it extends the man's vitality through its courage, strength and endurance; through his control, he demonstrates his mastery of heroic energy. Moreover, the cult of heroism, for instance, heroic poetry, is itself a defence, an aestheticisation of terror, since it glorifies violence. This military connotation is confirmed by the setting in our verse, where the mare is harnessed in Pharaoh's chariots.

As Marvin Pope remarks, mares are likely to cause disarray in battle, and in general steeds were stallions. The sex of the horse in our verse may primarily have been suggested by the sex of the Beloved, to whom the verse is addressed. The choice of a military image, and of a noble vigorous creature to describe the Beloved, however, induces a transfer of phallic energy, that in a woman is doubly threatening. A woman who is as powerful as a man endangers his supremacy; Pope gives many examples of this archetypal emasculating figure. An anomaly is a marked term, intensifying—through contrast—the attributes of its contradictory components. The mare in battle is terrifying, partially because it is so attractive.

The point, however, is that this energy contributes to royal display; in the poem it is diverted into the game of comparison. The mare is submissive; as an image for the Beloved, it hints at her proper subservience, as a member of the king's entourage, an adornment to his court, on whom he hangs his tropes and jewellery, the gold and silver pendants and chains of 1:10–11. Like the little sister in 8:8–10, she is beautified, and thereby concealed behind silver. "How beautiful are your cheeks in pendants" (1:10a). What is concealed is the freedom and wild delight of the mare, and the overwhelming attraction of nakedness.

If the last syllable of "lesusātî" be a first-person possessive suffix, then it increases the emphasis on her status as possession, which is allied to the king's self-satisfaction in these lines, and his wish to manipulate her according to his fancy.

With the last words, suddenly a sense of reality returns: "I have compared you, my love." The past (or perfect) tense reveals the inadequacy of all comparison, that is superseded by the truth. What is this truth? That she is "ra'yātî," my friend and equal. The epithets "ra'yâ" and "dôd" reduce all the personae to a simple human equation. The terms are both tautologous and separate, and in them aesthetic distance turns to human recognition:

הִנָּךְ יָפָה רַעְיָתִי הִנָּךְ יָפָה עֵינַיִךְ יוֹנִים:
הִנְּךָ יָפֶה דוֹדִי אַף נָעִים אַף־עַרְשֵׂנוּ רַעֲנָנָה:

([1:15] Behold, you are beautiful, my love, behold you are
beautiful; your eyes like doves.
[16] Behold you are beautiful, my love, yes, lovely; also our
bed is green.)

The Beloved looks from her loved one to the bed where they will
be united, in touch with and cradled by the verdant flourishing of nature.
The natural and human levels are metaphorically identified, and also log-
ically, as an image of the womb from which new life develops. The Lover
looks at his loved one's eyes, a mode of communication that precedes
language, and combines objectivity with an interchange of identity. Their
voices, moreover, merge into an inarticulate expression of wonder. Beauty
here is just set at a distance with the exclamation "hinnāk (There you
are!)"—and brought into relation through the twin terms *ra'yâ* and *dôd*.
They turn away from this marvellous gaze to the whole green world
between them, in which they unite. Out of this develops the language
of the poem, whose virtuosity, through enigma, ambiguity, and metaphor, returns us always to that first astonishment. The whole poem may
be seen as a giant tautology, repeating constantly "hinnāk yāpâ ra'yātî,
hinnekâ yāpēh dôdî (Behold you are beautiful, my love, Behold you are
beautiful, my love)," and the act of which no words can be spoken. And
out of this comes the creative flame that gives life to the spheres, natural,
human, linguistic, and divine.

CONCLUSION

The beauty of the world of the Song is the metaphorical equivalent
of the love of the lovers. Yet it comes from outside that world, and
threatens to subvert it. Beauty is a stranger, a gift, taking us by surprise,
wonderful and terrible; our civilisation devotes itself to being hospitable
to that gift, and controlling it. The transformation of beauty and its
resistance to change has been the subject of this chapter; in various forms
it is the basis of society, agricultural, pastoral, urban, commercial. Thus
it participates in and is the object of the creative process. Love shows
itself in beauty, that binds us to all things, in their autonomy. Aesthetic
experience is thus mystical experience; the message of the Song could be
expressed as "God is love, perceived in the beauty of the world." It comes
from the periphery to the centre, from the desert to the shrine and royal
bed; from lifelessness to where life is renewed. The stranger of 1:5 is the
city of 8:8–10 and the vineyard of 8:11–12, from which the king is

ambiguously excluded. It is then man who is in exile from beauty; it is beauty where he is most at home.

[Elsewhere] I shall be looking at the story of the Garden of Eden as the point where this exile began. In the Garden, Dionysiac beauty, and the enigma that goes with it, is incarnated in the serpent, the avatar of rational thought. As we have seen, beauty is a secondary articulation that exerts formal control over libidinal energy; the Garden is the scene of its precipitating trauma. The two forms of beauty, the beauty of intoxication and order, interact; there is a dialogue between the daughters of Jerusalem and the Beloved, and also a transformation, that is, from change to changelessness, darkness to whiteness, grapes to silver. Apollo has his chthonic voice, Dionysus his calm. Civilisation is founded on this transformation. Yet there is also a point of meeting between them, a relaxation of the ego; this is the Pastoral. The lovers look in each others' eyes and say "hinnāk yāpâ . . . hinnekâ yāpēh (Behold, you are beautiful . . . behold, you are beautiful)." The doves to which the eyes are compared fly to and fro. They are united in their love, and just apart; there is no desire, no tension between them. At this point beauty is not enigmatic, for there are no questions, merely the unquestionable "hinnāk . . . hinnekâ."

The Garden of Metaphor

Robert Alter

The Song of Songs comprises what are surely the most exquisite poems that have come down to us from ancient Israel, but the poetic principles on which they are shaped are in several ways instructively untypical of biblical verse. When it was more the scholarly fashion to date the book late, either in the Persian period or well into the Hellenistic period, these differences might have been attributed to changing poetic practices in the last centuries of biblical literary activity. Several recent analysts, however, have persuasively argued that all the supposed stylistic and lexical evidence for a late date is ambiguous, and it is quite possible, though not demonstrable, that these poems originated, whatever subsequent modifications they may have undergone, early in the First Commonwealth period.

The most likely sources of distinction between the Song of Songs and the rest of biblical poetry lie not in chronology but in genre, in purpose, and perhaps in social context. Although there are some striking love motifs elsewhere in biblical poetry—in Psalms, between man and God, in the Prophets, between God and Israel—the Song of Songs is the only surviving instance of purely secular love poetry from ancient Israel. The erotic symbolism of the Prophets would provide later ages an effective warrant for reading the Song of Songs as a religious allegory, but in fact the continuous celebration of passion and its pleasures makes this the most consistently secular of all biblical texts—even more so than Proverbs, which for all its pragmatic worldly concerns also stresses the fear of the Lord and the effect of divine justice on the here and now. We have

From *The Art of Biblical Poetry.* © 1985 by Robert Alter. Basic Books, 1985.

no way of knowing the precise circumstances under which or for which the Song of Songs was composed. A venerable and persistent scholarly theory sees it as the (vestigial?) liturgy of a fertility cult; others—to my mind, more plausibly—imagine it as a collection of wedding songs. What I should like to reject at the outset is the whole quest for the "life-setting" of the poems—because it is, necessarily, a will-o'-the-wisp and, even more, because it is a prime instance of the misplaced concreteness that has plagued biblical research, which naively presumes that the life-setting, if we could recover it, would somehow provide the key to the language, structure, and meaning of the poems.

The imagery of the Song of Songs is a curious mixture of pastoral, urban, and regal allusions, which leaves scant grounds for concluding whether the poems were composed among shepherds or courtiers or somewhere in between. References in rabbinic texts suggest that at least by the Roman period the poems were often sung at weddings, and, whoever composed them, there is surely something popular about these lyric celebrations of the flowering world, the beauties of the female and male bodies, and the delights of lovemaking. The Wisdom poetry of Job and Proverbs was created by members of what one could justifiably call the ancient Israelite intelligentsia. Prophetic verse was produced by individuals who belonged—by sensibility and in several signal instances by virtue of social background as well—to a spiritual-intellectual elite. The psalms were tied to the cult, and at least a good many of them were probably created in priestly circles (the mimetic example of short prayers embedded in biblical narrative suggests that ordinary people, in contradistinction to the professional psalm-poets, may have improvised personal prayers in simple prose). It is only in the Song of Songs that there is no one giving instruction or exhortation, no leader or hierophant, no memorializer of national experience, but instead the voices of two lovers, praising each other, yearning for each other, proffering invitations to enjoy. I shall not presume to guess whether these poems were composed by folk poets, but it is clear that their poetic idiom is one that, for all its artistic sophistication, is splendidly accessible to the folk, and that may well be the most plausible explanation for the formal differences from other kinds of biblical poetry.

To begin with, semantic parallelism is used here with a freedom one rarely encounters in other poetic texts in the Bible. Since virtually the whole book is a series of dramatic addresses between the lovers, this free gliding in and out of parallelism—the very antithesis of the neat boxing together of matched terms in Proverbs—may be dictated in part by the desire to give the verse the suppleness and liveliness of dramatic speech. Thus the very first line of the collection: "Let him kiss me with the kisses of his mouth, / for your love is better than wine" (1:2). The relation of the second verset to the first is not really parallelism but explanation—and a dramatically appropriate one at that, which is reinforced by the move from third person to second: your kisses, my love, are more delectable than wine, which is reason enough for me to have declared at large my desire for them.

In many lines, the second verset is a prepositional or adverbial modifier of the first verset—a pattern we have encountered occasionally elsewhere, but which here sometimes occurs in a whole sequence of lines, perhaps as part of an impulse to apprehend the elaborate and precious concreteness of the object evoked instead of finding a matching term for it. Here, for example, is the description of Solomon's royal palanquin:

1	Who is this coming up from the desert	like columns of smoke,
2	Perfumed with myrrh and frankincense	of all the merchant's powders?
3	Look, Solomon's couch,	sixty warriors round it
	of the warriors of Israel,	
4	All of them skilled with sword,	trained in war,
5	Each with sword on thigh,	for terror in the nights.
6	A litter King Solomon made him	of wood from Lebanon.
7	Its posts he made of silver,	its bolster gold,
	its cushion purple wool,	
8	Its inside decked with love	by the daughters of Jerusalem.

(3:6–10)

The only strictly parallelistic lines here are 4 and 7. For the rest, the poet seems to be reaching in his second (and third) versets for some further realization of the object, of what it is like, where it comes from: What surrounds Solomon's couch? Why are the warriors arrayed with their weapons? Who is it who has so lovingly upholstered the royal litter?

Now, the picture of a perfumed cloud ascending from the desert, with a splendid palanquin then revealed to the eye of the beholder, first with its entourage, afterward with its luxurious fixtures, also incorporates narrative progression; and because the collection involves the dramatic action of lovers coming together or seeking one another (though surely not, as some have fancied, in a formal drama), narrativity is the dominant pattern in a number of the poems. Such narrativity is of course in consonance with a general principle of parallelistic verse in the Bible, as one can see clearly in single lines like this: "Draw me after you, let us run— / the king has brought me to his chambers" (1:4). The difference is that in the Song of Songs there are whole poems in which all semblance of semantic equivalence between versets is put aside for the sake of narrative concatenation from verset to verset and from line to line. I will quote the nocturnal pursuit of the lover at the beginning of chapter 3 (3:1–4), with which one may usefully compare the parallel episode in 5:2–8 that works on the same poetic principle:

1	On my bed at night	I sought the one I so love,
	I sought him, did not find him.	
2	Let me rise and go round the town,	in the streets and squares
3	Let me seek the one I so love,	I sought him, did not find him.
4	The watchmen going round the town found me—	"Have you seen the one I so love?"
5	Scarce had I passed them	when I found the one I so love.
6	I held him, would not loose him,	till I brought him to my mother's house,
	to the chamber of her who conceived me.	

In this entire sequence of progressive actions, the only moment of semantic equivalence between versets is in the second and third versets of the last line, and the focusing movement there from house to chamber is subsumed under the general narrative pattern: the woman first gets a tight grip on her lover (6a), then brings him to her mother's house (6b), and finally introduces him (6c) into the chamber (perhaps the same one in which she was lying at the beginning of the sequence).

This brief specimen of narrative reflects two other stylistic peculiarities of the Song of Songs. Although the collection as a whole makes elaborate and sometimes extravagant use of figurative language, when narrative governs a whole poem, as in 3:1–4 and 5:2–8, figuration is entirely displaced by the report of sequenced actions. There are no metaphors or similes in these six lines, and, similarly, in the description of the palanquin coming up from the desert to Jerusalem that we glanced at, the only figurative language is "like columns of smoke" at the beginning (where the original reading may in fact have been "*in* columns of smoke") and "decked with love" at the end (where some have also seen a textual problem). The second notable stylistic feature of our poem is the prominence of verbatim repetition. Through the rapid narrative there is woven a thread of verbal recurrences that, disengaged, would sound like this: I sought the one I so love, I sought him, did not find him, let me seek the one I so love, I sought him, did not find him, the one I so love, I found the one I so love. This device has a strong affinity with the technique of incremental repetition that is reflected in the more archaic layers of biblical poetry (the most memorable instance being the Song of Deborah). In the Song of Songs, however, such repetition is used with a degree of flexibility one does not find in the archaic poems, and is especially favored in vocative forms where the lover adds some item of enraptured admiration to the repetition: "Oh, you are fair, my darling, / oh, you are fair, *your eyes are doves*" (4:1). One finds the increment as well in the explanatory note of a challenge: "How is your lover more than another, / fairest of women, / / how is your lover more than another, / *that thus you adjure us?*" (5:9). One notices that there is a sense of choreographic balance lacking in the simple use of incremental repetition because in both these lines an initial element ("my darling," "fairest of women") is subtracted as the increment is added. In any case, the closeness to incremental repetition is not necessarily evidence of an early date but might well reflect the more popular character of these love poems, folk poetry and its sophisticated derivatives being by nature conservative in their modes of expression.

The most telling divergence from quasi-synonymous parallelism in the Song of Songs is the use of one verset to introduce a simile and of the matching verset to indicate the referent of the simile: "Like a lily among brambles, / so is my darling among girls. / / Like an apple tree among forest trees, / so is my lover among lads" (2:2–3). The same pattern appears, with a very different effect, in some of the riddle-form proverbs. In the Song of Songs, such a pattern makes particular sense because, more than in any other poetic text of the Bible, what is at issue in the poems is the kind of transfers of meaning that take place when one thing is represented in terms of or through the image of something else, and the "like . . . / so . . ." formula aptly calls our attention to the operation of the simile. With the exception of the continuously narrative passages I have mentioned, figurative language plays a more prominent role here than anywhere else in biblical poetry, and the assumptions about how figurative language should be used have shifted in important respects.

The fact is that in a good deal of biblical poetry imagery serves rather secondary purposes, or sometimes there is not very much of it, and in any case "originality" of metaphoric invention would not appear to have been a consciously prized poetic value. Let me propose that outside the Song of Songs one can observe three general categories of imagery in biblical poems: avowedly conventional images, intensive images, and innovative images. Conventional imagery accounts for the preponderance of cases, and the book of Psalms is the showcase for the artful use of such stock images. Intensive imagery in most instances builds on conventional metaphors and similes, with the difference that a particular figure is pursued and elaborated through several lines or even a whole poem, so that it is given a kind of semantic amplitude or powerfully assertive pressure. Intensive imagery occurs sometimes in Psalms, fairly often in Job, and is the figurative mode par excellence of prophetic poetry. Innovative imagery is the rarest of the three categories, but it can occur from time to time in any genre of biblical verse simply because poetry is, among other things, a way of imagining the world through inventive similitude, and poets, whatever their conventional assumptions, may on occasion arrest the attention of their audience through an original or startling image. The highest concentration of innovative imagery in the Bible is evident in the book of Job, which I would take to be not strictly a generic matter but more a reflection of the poet's particular genius and his extraordinary ability to imagine disconcerting realities outside the frame of received wisdom and habitual perception. Let me offer some brief examples of all three categories of imagery in order to make this overview of biblical figuration more concrete, which in turn should help us see more clearly the striking difference of the Song of Songs.

Stock imagery, as I have intimated, is the staple of biblical poetry, and Psalms is the preeminent instance of its repeated deployment. Here is an exemplary line: "Guard me like the apple of Your eye, / in the shadow of Your wings conceal me" (Ps. 17:8). Both the apple of the eye as something to be cherished and the shadow of wings as a place of shelter are biblical clichés, though the two elements are interestingly connected here by a motif of darkness (the concentrated dark of the pupil and the extended shadow of wings) and linked in a pattern of intensification that moves from guarding to hiding. There may be, then, a certain effective orchestration of the semantic fields of the metaphors, but in regard to the purpose of the psalm, the advantage of working with such conventional figures is that our attention tends to be guided through the metaphoric vehicle to the tenor for which the vehicle was introduced. In fact, as Benjamin Hrushovski has recently argued, there is a misleading implication of unidirectional movement in those very terms *tenor* and *vehicle*, coined for critical usage by I. A. Richards some six decades ago, and when we return to the Song of Songs we will see precisely why the unidirectional model of metaphor is inappropriate. In the frequent biblical use, however, of stock imagery, the relation between metaphor and referent actually approaches that of a vehicle—that is, a mere "carrier" of meaning—to a tenor. In our line from Psalms, what the speaker, pleading for divine help, wants to convey is a sense of the tender protection he asks of God. The apple of the eye and the shading of wings communicate his feeling for the special care he seeks, but in their very conventionality the images scarcely have a life of their own. We think less about the dark of the eye and the shadow of wings than about the safeguarding from the Lord for which the supplicant prays.

Since I have pulled this line out of context, let me refer with a comment on the whole poem to the use of cliché in just one other fairly typical psalm, Psalm 94. In the twenty-three lines of this poem, which calls quite impressively on the Lord as a "God of retribution" to destroy His enemies, there are only four lines that contain any figurative language. How minimal and how conventional such language is will become clear by the quoting in sequence of these four isolated instances of figuration: "The Lord knows the designs of man, / that they are mere breath" (11); "until a pit is dug for the wicked" (13); "When I thought my foot had slipped, / Your faithfulness, Lord, supported me" (18); "But the Lord is my stronghold, / and my God is my sheltering rock" (22). Pitfall, stumbling, and stronghold occur time after time in biblical poetry, and their role in this otherwise nonfigurative poem is surely no more than a minor amplification of the idea that security depends upon God. The metaphor of breath or vapor may to the modern glance seem more striking, but it is in fact such a conventional designation for insubstantiality in the Bible that modern translations that render it unmetaphorically as "futile" do only small violence to the original.

We have seen [elsewhere] a number of instances of intensive imagery in our discussion of prophetic poetry and of structures of intensification, but since the focus of those considerations was not on figurative language, one brief example from the prophets may be useful. Here is Deutero-Isaiah elaborating a metaphor in order to contrast the ephemerality of humankind and the power and perdurability of God:

All flesh is grass,	all its faithfulness like the flower of the field.
Grass withers, flower fades	when the Lord's breath blows on them.
Grass withers, flower fades,	and the word of the Lord stands forever.
	(Isa. 40:6–8)

The metaphor of grass for transience is thoroughly conventional, but the poet gives it an intensive development through these three lines in the refrainlike repetition of the key phrases; the amplification of grass with flower (a vegetal figure that involves beauty and still more fragility and ephemerality, as flowers wither more quickly than grass); and in the contrast between grass and God's breath-wind-spirit (*ruaḥ*). God's power is a hot wind that makes transient growing things wither, but God's spirit is also the source of His promise to Israel, through covenant and prophecy, which will be fulfilled or "stand" (*yaqum*) forever while human things and human faithfulness vanish in the wilderness of time. One sees how a cliché has been transformed into poignantly evocative poetry, and here the frame of reference of the metaphor, ephemeral things flourishing, interpenetrates the frame of reference of Israel vis-à-vis God as the pitfalls and strongholds of Psalms do not do to the objects or ideas to which they allude.

Finally, the Job poet abundantly interweaves with such intensive developments of conventional figures forcefully innovative images that carry much of the burden of his argument. Sometimes the power of these images depends on an elaboration of their implications for two or three lines, as in this representation of human life as backbreaking day labor tolerable only because of the prospect of evening/death as surcease and recompense: "Has not man a term of service on earth, / and like the days of a hireling his days? / / Like a slave he pants for the shadows, / like a hireling he waits for his wage" (Job 7:1–2). Sometimes we find a rapid flow of innovative figures that in its strength from verset to verset seems quite Shakespearean, as in these images of the molding of man in the womb: "Did You not pour me out like milk, / curdle me like cheese? / / With skin and flesh You clothed me, / with bones and sinews wove me?" (Job 10:10–11). The brilliantly resourceful Job poet also offers a more compact version of the innovative image, in which an otherwise conventional term is endowed with terrific figurative power because of the context in which it is set. Thus, the verb *sabo'a*, "to be satisfied" or "sated," is extremely common in biblical usage, for the most part in literal or weakly figurative utterances, but this is how Job uses it to denounce the Friends: "Why do you pursue me like God, / and from my flesh you are not sated?" (Job 19:22). In context, especially since Job has just been talking about his bones sticking to his flesh and skin (19:20), the otherwise bland verb produces a horrific image of cannibalism, which manages to say a great deal with awesome compression about the perverted nature of the Friends' relationship to the stricken Job.

The innovative image by its forcefulness strongly colors our percep-

tion of its referent: once we imagine the Friends cannibalizing Job's dis-
eased and wasted flesh, we can scarcely dissociate the words they speak
and their moral intentions from this picture of barbaric violence. What
remains relatively stable, as in the two other general categories of biblical
imagery, is the subordinate relation of image to referent. We are never in
doubt that Job's subject is the Friends' censorious behavior toward him,
not cannibalism, or the shaping of the embryo, not cheese-making and
weaving. By contrast, what makes the Song of Songs unique among the
poetic texts of the Bible is that, quite often, imagery is given such full
and free play there that the lines of semantic subordination blur, and it
becomes a little uncertain what is illustration and what is referent.

It should be observed, to begin with, that in the Song of Songs the
process of figuration is frequently "foregrounded"—which is to say, as
the poet takes expressive advantage of representing something through
an image that brings out a salient quality it shares with the referent, he
calls our attention to his exploitation of similitude, to the artifice of
metaphorical representation. One lexical token of this tendency is that
the verbal root *d-m-h,* "to be like," or, in another conjugation, the tran-
sitive "to liken," which occurs only thirty times in the entire biblical
corpus (and not always with this meaning), appears five times in these
eight brief chapters of poetry, in each instance flaunting the effect of
figurative comparison. Beyond this lexical clue, the general frequency of
simile is itself a "laying bare" of the artifice, making the operation of
comparison explicit in the poem's surface structure.

The first occurrence of this verb as part of an ostentatious simile is
particularly instructive because of the seeming enigma of the image: "To
a mare among Pharaoh's chariots / I would liken you, my darling" (1:9).
Pharaoh's chariots were drawn by stallions, but the military stratagem
alluded to has been clearly understood by the commentators as far back
as the classical Midrashim: a mare in heat, let loose among chariotry,
could transform well-drawn battle lines into a chaos of wildly plunging
stallions. This is obviously an instance of what I have called innovative
imagery, and the poet—or, if one prefers, the speaker—is clearly inter-
ested in flaunting the innovation. The first verset gives us a startling
simile, as in the first half of a riddle-form proverb; the second verset
abandons semantic parallelism for the affirmation of simile making ("I
would liken you" or, perhaps, "I have likened you") together with the
specification in the vocative of the beloved referent of the simile. The
lover speaks out of a keen awareness of the power of figurative language

to break open closed frames of reference and make us see things with a shock of new recognition: the beloved in poem after poem is lovely, gentle, dovelike, fragrant; but the sexual attraction she exerts also has an almost violent power to drive males to distraction, as the equine military image powerfully suggests.

It is not certain whether the next two lines (1:10–11), which evoke the wreaths of jewels and precious metals with which the beloved should be adorned, are a continuation of the mare image (referring, that is, to ornaments like those with which a beautiful mare might be adorned) or the fragment of an unrelated poem. I would prefer to see these lines as an extension of the mare simile because that would be in keeping with a general practice in the Song of Songs of introducing a poetic comparison and then exploring its ramifications through several lines. A more clear-cut example occurs in these three lines (2:8–9), which also happen to turn on the next occurrence of the symptomatic verb *d-m-h:*

> Hark! My lover, here he comes! bounding over the mountains,
>   loping over the hills.
> My lover is like a buck or a young stag.
> Here he stands behind our wall, peering in at the windows,
>   peeping through the lattice.

This poem, which continues with the lover's invitation to the woman to come out with him into the vernal countryside, begins without evident simile: the waiting young woman simply hears the rapidly approaching footsteps of her lover and imagines him bounding across the hills to her home. What the middle line, which in the Hebrew begins with the verb of likening, *domeh,* does is to pick up a simile that has been pressing just beneath the verbal surface of the preceding line and to make it explicit—all the more explicit because the speaker offers overlapping alternatives of similitude, a buck *or* a young stag. The third line obviously continues the stag image that was adumbrated in the first line and spelled out in the second, but its delicate beauty is in part a function of the poised ambiguity as to what is foreground and what is background. It is easy enough to picture a soft-eyed stag, having come down from the hills, peering in through the lattice; it is just as easy to see the eager human lover, panting from his run, looking in at his beloved. The effect is the opposite of the sort of optical trick in which a design is perceived at one moment as a rabbit and the next as a duck but never as both at once, because through the magic of poetic likening the figure at the lattice is simultaneously stag and lover. What I would call the tonal consequence of this ambiguity is that the lover is entirely assimilated into the natural world at the same time that the natural world is felt to be profoundly in consonance with the lovers. This perfectly sets the stage for his invitation (2:10–13) to arise and join him in the freshly blossoming landscape, all winter rains now gone.

A variant of the line about the buck occurs in another poem at the end of the same chapter (2:16–17), and there is something to be learned from the different position and grammatical use of the verb of similitude:

> My lover is mine and I am his, who browses among the lilies.
> Until day breathes and shadows flee,
> Turn, and be you, my love, like a buck, or a young stag
> on the cleft mountains.

The verb *browses, ro‘eh,* which when applied to humans means "to herd" and would not make sense in that meaning here, requires a figurative reading from the beginning. The only landscape, then, in this brief poem is metaphorical: the woman is inviting her lover to a night of pleasure, urging him to hasten to enjoy to the utmost before day breaks. The lilies and the "cleft mountains"—others, comparing the line to 8:14, render this "mountains of spice," which amounts to the same erotic place—are on the landscape of her body, where he can gambol through the night. What is especially interesting in the light of our previous examples is that the verb of similitude occurs not in the speaker's declaration of likeness but in an imperative: "Be you, my love, like [*demeh le*] a buck." The artifice of poetry thus enters inside the frame of dramatic action represented through the monologue: the woman tells her man that the way he can most fully play the part of the lover is to be like the stag, to act out the poetic simile, feeding on these lilies and cavorting upon this mount of intimate delight.

Of the two other occurrences of the verb *d-m-h* in the Song of Songs, one is a variant of the line we have just considered, appearing at the very end of the book (8:14) and possibly detached from context. The other occurrence (7:7–9) provides still another instructive instance of how this poetry rides the momentum of metaphor:

> This stature of yours is like the palm, your breasts like the clusters.
> I say, let me climb the palm, let me hold its branches.
> Let your breast be like grape clusters, your breath like apples,
> Your palate like goodly wine flowing for my love smoothly,
> stirring the lips of sleepers.

The speaker first announces his controlling simile, proclaiming that his

beloved's stately figure is like (*damta le*) the palm. The second verset of
the initial line introduces a ramification—quite literally, a "branching
out"—of the palm image or, in terms of the general poetics of parallelism,
focuses it by moving from the tree to the fruit-laden boughs. The next
line is essentially an enactment of the simile, beginning with "I say,"
which Marvin Pope quite justifiably renders as "methinks" because the
verb equally implies intention and speech. The simile ceases to be an
"illustration" of some quality (the stately stature of the palm tree in the
woman) and becomes a reality that impels the speaker to a particular
course of action: if you are a palm, what is to be done with palm trees
is to climb them and enjoy their fruit. The last two lines of the poem
sustain the sense of a virtually real realm of simile by piling on a series
of images contiguous with the initial one but not identical with it: from
clusters of dates to grape clusters, from branches to apples, from the
breath of the mouth and from grapes to wine-sweet kisses.

Another reflection of the poetics of flaunted figuration that contributes to the distinctive beauty of the Song of Songs is the flamboyant
elaboration of the metaphor in fine excess of its function as the vehicle
for any human or erotic tenor. In terms of the semantic patterns of biblical
parallelism, this constitutes a special case of focusing, in which the second or third verset concretizes or characterizes a metaphor introduced in
the first verset in a way that shifts attention from the frame of reference
of the referent to the frame of reference of the metaphor. Let me quote
from the exquisite poem addressed to the dancing Shulamite in chapter 7
the vertical description of the woman, ascending from feet to head
(7:1–5).

1 How lovely your feet in sandals,   nobleman's daughter!
2 Your curving thighs are like   the work of a master's hand.
   ornaments,

3 Your sex a rounded bowl—   may it never lack mixed wine!
4 Your belly a heap of wheat,   hedged about with lilies.
5 Your two breasts like two fawns,   twins of a gazelle.
6 Your neck like an ivory tower,   your eyes pools in Heshbon
              by the gate of Bat-Rabbim.
7 Your nose like the tower of David,   looking out toward Damascus.
8 Your head on you like crimson   the locks of your head like purple,
   wool,
              a king is caught in the flowing tresses.

This way of using metaphor will seem peculiar only if one insists upon imposing on the text the aesthetic of a later age. A prime instance of what I have called the misplaced concreteness of biblical research is that proponents of the theory of a fertility-cult liturgy have felt that the imagery of metallic ornament had to be explained as a reference to the statuette of a love goddess and the looming architectural imagery by an invoking of the allegedly supernatural character of the female addressed. This makes only a little more sense than to claim that when John Donne in "The Sunne Rising" writes, "She is all States, and all Princes, I, / Nothing else is," he must be addressing, by virtue of the global imagery, some cosmic goddess and not sweet Ann Donne.

Our passage begins without simile for the simple technical reason that the second verset of line 1 is used to address the woman who is the subject of the enraptured description. After this point, the second (or, for the triadic lines, the third) verset of each line is employed quite consistently to flaunt the metaphor by pushing its frame of reference into the foreground. The poet sets no limit on and aims for no unity in the semantic fields from which he draws his figures, moving rapidly from artisanry to agriculture to the animal kingdom to architecture, and concluding with dyed textiles. (In the analogous vertical description of the lover, 5:10–16, the imagery similarly wanders from doves bathing in watercourses and beds of spices to artifacts of gold, ivory, and marble, though the semantic field of artifact dominates as the celebration of the male body concentrates on the beautiful hardness of arms, thighs, and loins.) There is nevertheless a tactical advantage in beginning the description with perfectly curved ornaments and a rounded bowl or goblet, for the woman's beauty is so exquisite that the best analogue for it is the craft of the master artisan, an implicit third term of comparison being the poet's fine craft in so nicely matching image with object for each lovely aspect of this body.

That implied celebration of artifice may explain in part the flamboyant elaboration of the metaphors in all the concluding versets. It should be observed, however, that the function of these elaborations changes from line to line in accordance with both the body part invoked and the position of the line in the poem. In line 2, "the work of a master's hand" serves chiefly as an intensifier of the preceding simile of ornament and as a way of foregrounding the idea of artifice at the beginning of the series. In lines 3–5, as the description moves upward from feet and thighs to the central erogenous zone of vagina, belly, and breasts, the elaborations of the metaphor in the second versets are a way of being at once sexually explicit and decorous through elegant *double entente*. That is, we are meant to be continuously aware of the sexual details referred to, but it is the wittily deployed frame of reference of the metaphor that is kept in the foreground of our vision: we know the poet alludes to the physiology of lovemaking, but we "see" a curved bowl that never runs dry; the wheatlike belly bordered by a hedge of lilies is an ingenious superimposition of an agricultural image on an erotic one, since lilies elsewhere are implicitly associated with pubic hair; the bouncing, supple, symmetrical breasts are not just two fawns but also, in the focusing elaboration, a gazelle's perfectly matched twins.

The geographical specifications of the final versets in lines 6 and 7 have troubled many readers. It seems to me that here, when the poet has moved above the central sexual area of the body, he no longer is impelled to work out a cunning congruity between image and referent by way of *double entente,* and instead he can give free rein to the exuberance of figurative elaboration that in different ways has been perceptible in all the previous metaphors. If, as his eye moves to neck and face, the quality of grandeur rather than supple sexual allure is now uppermost, there is a poetic logic in the speaker's expanding these images of soaring architectural splendor and making the figurative frame of reference so prominent that we move from the dancing Shulamite to the public world of the gate at Bat-Rabbim and the tower of Lebanon looking toward Damascus. As the lover's gaze moves up from the parts of the body usually covered and thus seen by him alone to the parts generally visible, it is appropriate that the similes for her beauty should be drawn now from the public realm. In a final turn, moreover, of the technique of last-verset elaboration, the triadic line 8 introduces an element of climactic surprise: the Shulamite's hair having been compared to brilliantly dyed wool or fabric, we discover that a king is caught, or bound, in the tresses (the Hebrew for this last term is a little doubtful, but since the root suggests running motion, the reference to flowing hair in context seems probable). This amounts to a strong elaboration of a relatively weak metaphor, and an elaboration that subsumes the entire series of images that has preceded: the powerful allure of sandaled feet, curving thighs, and all the rest that has pulsated through every choice of image now culminates in the hair, where at last the lover, through the self-designation of king, introduces himself into the poem, quite literally interinvolves himself with the beloved ("a king is caught in the flowing tresses"). Up till now, she has been separate from him, dancing before his eager eye. Now, after a climactic line summarizing her beauty (7:7), he goes on to imagine embracing her and enjoying her (7:8–10, the climbing of the palm tree that

I quoted earlier). It is a lovely illustration of how the exuberant metaphors carry the action forward.

Such obtrusions of metaphorical elaboration are allied with another distinctive mode of figuration of these poems, in which the boundaries between figure and referent inside and outside, human body and accoutrement or natural setting, become suggestively fluid. Let me first cite three lines from the brief poem at the end of chapter 1 (1:12–14):

While the king was on his couch,	my nard gave off its scent.
A sachet of myrrh is my lover to me,	between my breasts he lodges.
A cluster of cypress is my lover to me,	in the vineyards of Ein Gedi.

The first line is without figuration, the woman simply stating that she has scented her body for her lover. But the immediately following metaphoric representation of the lover as a sachet of myrrh—because he nestles between her breasts all night long—produces a delightful confusion between the literal nard with which she has perfumed herself and the figurative myrrh she cradles in her lover. Thus the act and actors of love become intertwined with the fragrant paraphernalia of love. The third line offers an alternative image of a bundle of aromatic herbs and then, in the second verset, one of those odd geographical specifications like those we encountered in our preceding text. I have not followed the New JPS [Jewish Publication Society] and Marvin Pope in translating the second verset as "from the vineyards," because it seems to me that the Hebrew has an ambiguity worth preserving. Presumably the metaphor is elaborated geographically because the luxuriant oasis at Ein Gedi was especially known for its trees and plants with aromatic leaves, and so the specification amounts to a heightening of the original assertion. At the same time the initial Hebrew particle *be,* which usually means "in," leaves a teasing margin for imagining that it is not the cypress cluster that *comes from* Ein Gedi but the fragrant embrace of the lovers that takes place *in* Ein Gedi. Though this second meaning is less likely, it is perfectly consistent with the syntax of the line, and the very possibility of this construal makes it hard to be sure where the metaphor stops and the human encounter it represents begins. There is, in other words, an odd and satisfying consonance in this teasing game of transformations between the pleasure of play with language through metaphor and the pleasure of love play that is the subject of the lines. That same consonance informs the beautiful poem that takes up all of chapter 4, ending in the first verse of chapter 5. It will provide an apt concluding illustration of the poetic art of the Song of Songs.

1 Oh, you are fair, my darling,   oh, you are fair, your eyes are doves.

2 Behind your veil, your hair like a flock of goats   streaming down Mount Gilead.

3 Your teeth are like a flock of ewes   coming up from the bath,

4 Each one bearing twins,   none bereft among them.

5 Like the scarlet thread your lips,   your mouth is lovely.

6 Like a pomegranate-slice your brow   behind your veil.

7 Like the tower of David your neck,   built in rows.

8 A thousand shields are hung on it,   all the heroes' bucklers.

9 Your two breasts are like two fawns,   twins of the gazelle,

        browsing among the lilies.

10 Until day breathes   and shadows flee

11 I'll betake me to the mount of myrrh   and to the hill of frankincense.

12 You are all fair, my darling,   there's no blemish in you.

13 With me from Lebanon, bride,   with me from Lebanon, come!

14 Descend from Amana's peak,   from the peak of Senir and Hermon,

15 From the dens of lions,   from the mounts of panthers.

16 You ravish my heart, bride,   you ravish my heart with one glance of your eyes,

        with one gem of your necklace.

17 How fair your love, my sister and bride,   how much better your love than wine,

        and the scent of your ointments than any spice!

18 Nectar your lips drip, bride,   honey and milk under your tongue,

        and the scent of your robes like Lebanon's scent.

19 A locked garden, my sister and bride,   a locked pool, a sealed-up spring.

20 Your groove a grove of pomegranates   with luscious fruit,

        cypress with nard.

21 Nard and saffron, cane and cinnamon,   with all aromatic woods,

22 Myrrh and aloes,   with all choice perfumes.

23 A garden spring,   a well of fresh water,
                        flowing from Lebanon.
24 Stir, north wind,   come, south wind,
25 Breathe on my garden,   let its spices flow.
26 "Let my lover come to his   and eat its luscious fruit."
     garden,
27 I've come to my garden, my   I've plucked my myrrh with my
     sister and bride,   spice,
28 Eaten my honeycomb with my   drunk my wine with my milk.
     honey,
29 "Eat, friends, and drink,   be drunk with love."

As elsewhere in the Song of Songs, the poet draws his images from whatever semantic fields seem apt for the local figures—domesticated and wild animals, dyes, food, architecture, perfumes, and the floral world. Flamboyant elaboration of the metaphor, in which the metaphoric image takes over the foreground, governs the first third of the poem (lines 2–4, 7–9), culminating in the extravagant picture of the woman's neck as a tower hung with shields. The very repetition of *ke* ("like"), the particle of similitude, half a dozen times through these initial lines, calls attention to the activity of figurative comparison as it is being carried out. There is a certain witty ingenuity with which the elaborated metaphors are related to the body parts: twin-bearing, newly washed ewes to two perfect rows of white teeth and, perhaps, shields on the tower walls recalling the layered rows of a necklace.

What I should like to follow out more closely, however, is the wonderful transformations that the landscape of fragrant mountains and gardens undergoes from line 11 to the end of the poem. The first mountain and hill—rarely has a formulaic word-pair been used so suggestively—in line 11 are metaphorical, referring to the body of the beloved or, perhaps, as some have proposed, more specifically to the *mons veneris*. It is interesting that the use of two nouns in the construct state to form a metaphor ("mount of myrrh," "hill of frankincense") is quite rare elsewhere in biblical poetry, though it will become a standard procedure in postbiblical Hebrew poetry. The naturalness with which the poet adopts that device here reflects how readily objects in the Song of Songs are changed into metaphors. The Hebrew for "frankincense" is *levonah*, which sets up an intriguing *faux raccord* with "Lebanon," *levanon*, two lines down. From the body as landscape—an identification already adumbrated in the comparison of hair to flocks coming down from the mountain and teeth to ewes coming up from the washing—the poem moves to an actual landscape with real rather than figurative promontories. If domesticated or in any case gentle animals populate the metaphorical landscape at the beginning, there is a new note of danger or excitement in the allusion to the lairs of panthers and lions on the real northern mountainside. The repeated verb "ravish" in line 16, apparently derived from *lev*, "heart," picks up in its sound (*libavtini*) the interecho of *levonah* and *levanon* and so triangulates the body-as-landscape, the external landscape, and the passion the beloved inspires.

The last thirteen lines of the poem, as the speaker moves toward the consummation of love intimated in lines 26–29, reflect much more of an orchestration of the semantic fields of the metaphors: fruit, honey, milk, wine, and, in consonance with the sweet fluidity of this list of edibles, a spring of fresh flowing water and all the conceivable spices that could grow in a well-irrigated garden. Lebanon, which as we have seen has already played an important role in threading back and forth between the literal and figurative landscapes, continues to serve as a unifier. The scent of the beloved's robes is like Lebanon's scent (line 18), no doubt because Lebanon is a place where aromatic trees grow, but also with the suggestion, again fusing figurative with literal, that the scent of Lebanon clings to her dress because she has just returned from there (lines 13–15). "All aromatic woods" in line 21 is literally in the Hebrew "all the trees of *levonah*," and the echo of *levonah-levanon* is carried forward two lines later when the locked spring in the garden wells up with flowing water (*nozlim*, an untranslatable poetic synonym for water) from Lebanon—whether because Lebanon, with its mountain streams, is the superlative locus of fresh running water, or because one is to suppose some mysterious subterranean feed-in from the waters of wild and mountainous Lebanon to this cultivated garden. In either case, there is a suggestive crossover back from the actual landscape to a metaphorical one. The garden at the end that the lover enters—and to "come to" or "enter" often has a technical sexual meaning in biblical Hebrew—is the body of the beloved, and one is not hard put to see the physiological fact alluded to in the fragrant flowing of line 25 (the same root as *nozlim* in line 23) that precedes the enjoyment of luscious fruit.

What I have just said, however, catches only one side of a restless dialectic movement of signification and as such darkens the delicately nuanced beauty of the poem with the shadow of reductionism. For though we know, and surely the original audience was intended to know, that the last half of the poem conjures up a delectable scene of love's consummation, this garden of aromatic plants, wafted by the gentle winds, watered by a hidden spring, is in its own right an alluring presence to the imagination before and after any decoding into a detailed set of sexual allusions. The poetry by the end becomes a kind of self-transcendence of *double entente:* the beloved's body is, in a sense, "represented" as a garden, but it also turns into a real garden, magically continuous with the mountain landscape so aptly introduced at the midpoint of the poem.

It is hardly surprising that only here in biblical poetry do we encounter such enchanting interfusions between the literal and metaphorical realms, because only here is the exuberant gratification of love through all five senses the subject. Prevalent preconceptions about the Hebrew Bible lead us to think of it as a collection of writings rather grimly committed to the notions of covenant, law, solemn obligation, and thus the very antithesis of the idea of play. There is more than a grain of truth in such preconceptions (one can scarcely imagine a Hebrew Aristophanes or a Hebrew *Odyssey*), but the literary art of the Bible, in both prose narrative and poetry, reflects many more elements of playfulness than might meet the casual eye. Only in the Song of Songs, however, is the writer's art directed to the imaginative realization of a world of uninhibited self-delighting play, without moral conflict, without the urgent context of history and nationhood and destiny, without the looming perspectives of a theological worldview. Poetic language and, in particular, its most characteristic procedure, figuration, are manipulated as pleasurable substance: metaphor transforms the body into spices and perfumes, wine and luscious fruit, all of which figurative images blur into the actual setting in which the lovers enact their love, a natural setting replete with just those delectable things. There is a harmonious correspondence between poem and world, the world exhibiting the lovely tracery of satisfying linkages that characterizes poetry itself. In the fluctuating movement from literal to figurative and back again, both sides of the dialectic are enhanced: the inventions of the poetic medium become potently suffused with the gratifying associations of the erotic, and erotic longing and fulfillment are graced with the elegant aesthetic form of a refined poetic art.

The Song of Songs in Early Jewish Mysticism

Arthur Green

For my friend Bob Cover: The lecture he never got to hear.
Ḥaval al d'avdin!

Of all the metaphors for the divine/human relationship which the Jewish mystics inherited from the earlier, exoteric Jewish tradition, none was more central to them than that of the Divine Bridegroom and Israel as his beloved spouse. God as lover of Israel had shared center stage in the early rabbinic imagination with God as father and king, the twin images of divine transcendence most generally associated in later times with the religious language of Judaism. With the contraction of midrashic thinking in the Middle Ages and its displacement by philosophical theology as the dominant Jewish way of speaking about God, the traditions of sacred eros, scandalous to the philosophers, became virtually the unique legacy of the mystics. As though to spite their philosophical opponents, the Kabbalists—as Jewish mystics were called from the thirteenth century— developed an erotic mythology that would shock not only the respectable Maimonidean, but even the earlier and more daring midrashic masters themselves.

The biblical basis for talk of a love affair or marriage between the Creator and the people of Israel is in fact rather meager: not a mention in the Torah itself, and a somewhat sparse collection of passages from Hosea, Isaiah and Jeremiah, a good many of which spoke of God's marriage to his people in order to chide Israel for her unfaithfulness rather than to praise her or to extol the match. These passages were enhanced,

---

From *Orim* 2, no. 2 (Spring 1987). © 1987 by Arthur Green.

indeed overwhelmed at a rather early date, by the "evidence" of the Song of Songs. This witness, however, to the love of God and Israel, was not without its problems.

The debate as to the original *Sitz im Leben* of those poems which constitute the biblical Song of Songs is not yet concluded. Some have chosen to read these poems much as the biblical text itself seems to present them: a series of love, courtship and marriage poems between shepherd and shepherdess. Other, perhaps more penetrating readers, see the Canticle as a somewhat more sophisticated and urban literary product rather than as a collection of country folk songs. The references to the tower of David and the daughters of Jerusalem, perhaps even to the Solomonic superscription, are but the beginning points of this reading. The text is seen as too artful, too conscious of its own rhythms, too lavish in its use of metaphor to be a randomly strung together group of traditional songs.

But the real debate over the Canticle's origin is that which concerns its purported cultic background. Love poetry of this sophistication, so the argument goes, could only have existed in a cultic context in the ancient Near East. Shepherd and shepherdess are, in one way or another, god and goddess or deity and consort. Of course, ancient Near Eastern gods do fall in love with human females and vice versa, so one partner or the other in a particular poem may indeed be a mortal, and mortals may have dramatically acted out one or both roles in the cultic performance in which the poems were set. But the poems themselves, so exultant and unabashed in their celebration of eros, could not be other than a part of that erotically charged and fertility-centered Canaanite religion that was such anathema to the prophets of Israel.

Each side in this debate will of course be able to adduce its parallel sources and ancient witnesses. But those who choose to view the song as a cultic product will have on their side, albeit obliquely, the rather surprising support of rabbi Akiba ben Joseph, the leading rabbinic teacher and theologian of the early second century. The canonicity of the Canticle was still being debated in Akiba's time, and it was he who insisted on its inclusion with the now classical formulation: "The whole world is not worthy of the day the Song of Songs was given to Israel, for all of Scripture is (or all the Songs are) holy, but the Song of Songs is the Holy of Holies."

What did Akiba have in mind? Clearly it was not just romance; love was indeed a supreme value in Akiba's religious worldview, but it was hardly the erotic passions of that country shepherd's existence which he himself had abandoned that he extols here as the "Holy of Holies." For Akiba it was clear that the Song of Songs is a holy book, which is to say that its verses describe a love that involves the deity. Since Akiba's God is the singular and essentially masculine figure of the biblical and rabbinic traditions, it seems fair to say that the Song, from Akiba's point of view, is about the love between that God and his beloved consort, bride or spouse, whoever that may be. It is in this sense that Akiba—with the later synagogue and church fully behind him—lends support to the view that the Song of Songs is sacred or cultic in its original or "true" meaning. Unable to retain the old pagan names or references to cultic practice, the shapers of the canon knew, perhaps instinctively, that this was a sacred poem, and as such preserved it, though denuded of such references in the moment it was frozen into the biblical text it does have a surprisingly "secular" appearance. By Akiba's day, battles with the ancient cults of Palestine long won and forgotten, a new pair of names, *qadosh barukh hu* and *yisra'el,* could be assigned to these ancient and properly revered verses of sacred eros.

We all know, of course, that the rabbis read the Song as a love poem between God and the Community of Israel. The best witness to this reading is the Targum, here very much an extended Aramaic paraphrase of the Song—as was required—rather than a translation. The Targumist's reading is primarily a historical one, in which the verses of the Song recount the narrative of Israel's redemption from Egypt, standing before "her" God at Sinai, wandering through the wilderness, coming into the Promised Land, building the Temple, sinning with other gods, being cast out, and again awaiting God's redemption. There is something quite reductive about the spelling out of God and Israel's love in such full historic detail. "Thy two breasts" as "the two tablets of the law" or as "Moses and Aaron" does leave something to be desired in the realm of literary eros.

The late Saul Lieberman has claimed, however, that this historical allegory was, to Akiba and his circle, merely the exoteric reading of the most sacred Song. Noting that Akiba spoke of the day when the Song of Songs was *given* to Israel, a term otherwise applied only to the Torah itself, Lieberman shows the early rabbis to have believed in the revelation of the Song, spoken by the angels or by God himself and revealed to Israel in a moment of theophany, either at the splitting of the Sea or at the foot of Sinai, one of those two moments when God descended in his chariot and was actually seen by the Community of Israel. Another statement of Akiba's (though preserved in somewhat garbled form) says that "had the Torah not been given to Israel, the Song of Songs would have sufficed for the conduct of the world"—indeed a rather intriguing possibility.

Akiba seems to belong to those who see Sinai as the setting of the Song, and the Song itself as the crown of that great apocalyptic moment when the heavens opened and all of Torah—primordial, written, oral, and yet to be developed—was brought forth. Eliezer ben Hyrcanus, a leading scholar of the generation before Akiba, assigned it rather to the Sea. This may be related to the midrashic tradition that sees God as having revealed himself as a wise and elderly judge at Sinai, but as a young warrior for the defeat of the Egyptians—each according to the moment's needs. Surely the God of Canticles is the youthful figure, not the elder. (Jewish ritual practice, incidentally, follows Eliezer's view, assigning the reading of the Song to the latter days of Passover.) The sages seem to agree, however, that the esoteric meaning of the Song is a description of the body of God as seen by Israel in the moment of revelation: the lover, described so passionately limb by limb, is the Holy One as Israel saw him. No wonder they forbade the public teaching of this esoteric midrash! The love dialogue between God and Israel, properly understood, was not a recounting of Jewish history, but an erotic hymn in which divine lover and earthly beloved whispered to one another descriptions of secret and intimate beauty.

This midrash, as Lieberman further shows, was the exegetical context for what became known as *shi'ur qomah shel yotzer bereshit,* the measurement of the Creator's form. In a series of fragments preserved amid the Hekhalot sources (early "Palace" mysticism), gigantic measurements of the limbs of the divine body are offered, entirely unaccompanied by explanation. This speculative tradition, so Lieberman claims, grows directly out of that midrash which stated:

> His Head is a Gold Diadem (Cant. 5:10)—this is the King of Kings who appeared to Israel in many images. Doing battle with Pharoah at the Sea He appeared as a youth, because a youth is fitting to battle . . . and just as they saw Him, as it were, so too they saw the *Merkavah* which had come down to the sea.

The *shi'ur qomah* tradition, preserved by the Near Eastern rabbis into the early Middle Ages, was vigorously denounced by the rationalist Maimonides, dismissed as the creation of some Roman preacher and surely not of the Sages. It was the Kabbalists who were able, in the face of the

Maimonidean denunciation, to preserve it. When Maimonides proclaimed in his Code, "One who says that God has a body or a depictable form is a heretic," rabbi Abraham ben David of Posquières, the earliest figure to be associated with Kabbalistic tradition, replied in a gloss, "Greater and better persons than he believed it." This shi'ur qomah tradition, however imperfectly preserved or understood by the time of its twelfth-century migration to Languedoc, provided justification (and perhaps impetus as well) for the strong erotic current in the Kabbalists' own theosophical speculations, including a prominent new role they gave to their reading of the Song of Songs.

II

Writing at a very late date in the history of Kabbalistic exegesis, Elisha Gallico of Safed (late sixteenth century) says that he knows of four readings of the Canticle, to which he hopes to add a fifth. The four he knows are:

A first reading in which "the Community of Israel longs for and seeks out her lover and He responds in kind"—presumably the midrashic reading;

a second one relating to "the Torah and its students," where the Song concerns "the desire of students to attain to Torah, both hidden and revealed." This he rightly ascribes to a recent innovation, the commentary *Ayelet Ahavim* by his compatriot Solomon Alqabets;

a third in which "intellect and matter" are the loving pair, or an Aristotelian reading; and

a fourth in which "the soul, drawn from beneath the throne of God, longs to return to the spiritual delights of her master's home, in which she delighted before her descent into this world," or the Neoplatonic.

What then has become of Kabbalistic exegesis? Can it be that this latter-day Kabbalist ignores the contribution of that tradition in which he stands? Did the Kabbalists add nothing to the interpretation of the Canticle? Far from it. As they did in many areas, the Kabbalists entered into the mainstream of rabbinic exegesis and proclaimed it their own. Like the early rabbis, the Kabbalists claimed that the Song was about the love between the Blessed Holy One and *knesset yisra'el,* the Community of Israel—but with a difference. For the Kabbalist, the "Community of Israel" no longer designates a human group in its primary meaning, but refers to the *Shekhinah,* the feminine-receptive element within the Godhead, designated elsewhere as Kingdom, Jerusalem, Temple, Sabbath,

Moon, Sea, Bride, Glory, and a myriad of other symbolic terms. To say it in a nutshell (a well-known Kabbalistic appellation for the guarding of mystery), medieval Jewish esotericism sees the *hieros gamos* (divine wedding) taking place *within* God, rather than between God and Israel. This development is made possible by the major innovation in Kabbalistic thought, the *sefirot,* symbol-laden stages in the divine self-revelation. The static unity of God, a cornerstone of Jewish philosophy, is converted by the Kabbalists into a dynamic unity of one-in-ten. The ten sefirot are bound to and leap forth from the One, in the words of a widely used image, "like a flame attached to a coal," having all the irregularity and yet the unity of the multiple darting tongues of a single fire.

The essential subject matter of all Kabbalistic teaching is an account of this pulsating inner life of divinity: how the hidden One, beyond all description, takes on the multiple garments of God as we know him— and in this case we do well to add—and her. God the lover, warrior, judge, king, father, mother, son, daughter, all have particular loci in the sefirotic system. As already indicated, personal metaphors by no means exhaust the Kabbalists' store: the Zohar, the greatest work of Spanish Kabbalah, seems to give as much play to images of light and water as it does to those of person. To use the water imagery for a moment, we may say that the most hidden levels of divinity are described as "the depths of the well." At the surface of this well there bubbles forth a spring, and thence there proceed six intertwining rivers, all of which ultimately flow into the sea, or the Shekhinah. The tenth *sefirah* thus represents the divine fullness, the energy of God at the crest of its flow, ready to spill over into the lower worlds.

But the sefirot are used not only to describe the orderly and uninterrupted flow of divine energy into the world. The myth of evil, that which causes the flow to cease, is an essential part of the Kabbalistic system; through it elements of alienation, emptiness and longing are added to the picture of divinity. The link between the Shekhinah and the upper nine stages of divinity is broken by the power of human sin, the this-worldly embodiment of cosmic evil. Only human goodness in the form of fulfillment of God's commandments can reestablish the broken connection, bringing the Shekhinah back into the good graces of her spouse and restoring some measure of divine presence to the lower worlds as well. In this drama of alternating longing and fulfillment within God, it is easy to see that the Canticle will have a major role to play.

> Upon my couch at night
> I sought the one I love—

I sought, but found him not.
"I must rise and roam the town,
Through the streets and through the squares;
I must seek the one I love."
I sought but found him not.
I met the watchmen
Who patrol the town.
"Have you seen the one I love?"
Scarcely had I passed them
When I found the one I love.
I held him fast, I would not let him go
Till I brought him to my mother's house,
To the chamber of her who conceived me.

(Song of Songs 3:1–4)

Who are we latter-day readers to tell the Kabbalist that the real subject of this passage is some obscure shepherd girl who has stumbled into Solomon's Jerusalem, rather than the eternal mythic female ever longing for the renewed espousals of her youth?

The first Kabbalist to comment on the Song of Songs, rabbi Ezra ben Solomon of Gerona, composed in about 1250 a commentary often ascribed to his more famous contemporary, Moses Nahmanides. He prefaces his commentary with a brief lexicon, a list of terms which, as he tells the reader, you will find in no dictionary. "Lebanon," "wine" and "spice," he tells us, all refer to *Ḥokhmah*, the second of the ten sefirot and the most recondite of which we may speak. "Apple" and "garden" both refer to the Glory or Shekhinah, while "lily," with its six petals, refers to the six intermediary channels. He also warns us—perhaps because he knew our generation was to come—against overinterpretation: many verses in the Song, he says, are there simply to carry out the imagery begun elsewhere, and for no other purpose. This rather conservative exegetical declaration was ignored by most of rabbi Ezra's Kabbalistic successors.

The work is called "Song of Songs," he tells us, because in the words of Psalm 19, "Day unto day utters speech"; this Song is sung by each of the divine "days" or sefirot, beginning with the lowest, Throne or Glory, and culminating with Ḥokhmah above. Thus the Sages have described the Canticle as "that song which God sings each day." As an example of rabbi Ezra's exegesis, we may quote his reading of the opening verse, "Let Him kiss me":

The words of the Glory, desiring longingly to ascend, to cleave
to that sublime and unequalled light. The ascent is one of mind
and thought, and thus is spoken of in a hidden manner (i.e.,
in the third person). The kiss symbolizes the joy of the soul's
attachment to the source of life . . . "for your kisses are
sweeter than wine": read: are sweet when from wine, and
emanated light increases when it comes from wine, the wisdom of God's "I," the rung of sublime light (*Hokhmah*), to
which all desire to cleave and ascend. "Are good" (in the
plural) refers to the abundance of sublime light that is divided
and sparkles forth in every direction, as Scripture says, "When
he kindles (*be'hetivo*) the light" and "God saw the light, that
it was good."

The association here of devotional and sefirotic mysticism is typical
of Ezra's work. The "Glory" here is the devoted bride whose longings
for union with her spouse also represent the longing of the worshipper's
soul for reunion with God.

Ezra's immediate successor in the Kabbalistic exegesis of Canticles
was Isaac Ibn Sahula, who lived in the Castilian town of Guadalajara and
wrote during the 1280s. Ibn Sahula is primarily known to the student of
Hebrew literature as the author of *Meshal haKadmoni,* an erudite and witty
collection of fables and morality tales that achieved considerable popular-
ity in the later Middle Ages. He lived in the same town as the author of
the Zohar, whom we shall discuss presently, and his works contain the
earliest known quotations from the Zohar literature, an important link
in Gershom Scholem's masterful detective work a generation ago in con-
clusively assigning that work's authorship. Sahula's only other preserved
work, surprisingly unpublished until now, is his commentary on Canticles, which survives in but a single Oxford manuscript.

Sahula's approach to the text is a two-pronged one; he uses the by
now widely accepted notion that a text may be—nay, must be—read on
both hidden and revealed levels. His esoteric commentary remains, even
after careful reading, just that. Believing that the mysteries of the sefirot
should not be revealed to the uninitiated, Sahula's references are short,
elliptical and often obscure. He will interpret one verse simply by quoting
another, leaving it to the experienced reader of Kabbalistic lore to put the
two together and come out with some—hopefully the intended—referent
to esoteric teaching.

On "the kisses of his mouth" he says, in a lovely rhymed Hebrew couplet: "I have heard that there is an awesome secret to the word 'His mouth,' a powerful staff, a rod of beauty. And who knows whether his mouth and his heart are in accord, encouraging the humble?" From parallel comments elsewhere, especially in the Zohar, and from a general familiarity with Kabbalistic rhetoric, we can make an educated guess that "mouth" here is being read as the Shekhinah, a "powerful staff" because of her associations with the left (or judging) side of God, but here held in the hand of *Tiferet* or Beauty, the essential masculine principle within divinity. Tiferet, located at the center of the Kabbalistic diagram, is also often called "Heart," so that the accord of mouth and heart probably refers to the union of these two, or at least to the uplifting of the Shekhinah so that she can be on the same rung as her spouse. All of this involves a certain amount of guesswork on the part of the reader. This may be why, after all, Sahula's manuscript never found a publisher.

If the esoteric commentary is hard to decipher, however, the exoteric interpretation is a source of real delight. Here Sahula makes generous use of his considerable urbanity and literary skill. For him, the "plain" meaning of the Song of Songs is what can best be characterized as devotional: it is an allegory of the eternal human striving for perfection, identical, in his reading, with the longing of the ideal soul for the blessed presence or Shekhinah of God. On this level he is willing to speak quite openly about "the kisses of his mouth":

> Our sages have already informed us about the rung of the "kiss" in telling us concerning the verse "Moses the servant of the Lord died there by the mouth of God" (Deut. 34:5) that he died by a kiss. This being the case, we know what a high rung the kiss must be, that by which Moses our master passed from this transitory and fleeting life into life eternal. Then too there is a tradition claiming that Moses did not die at all, but ascended and serves in heaven. This kiss would be a flowing forth of spirit from its source. . . . Even speaking in a revealed manner we may say that the kiss represents the beginning of thought and the end of deed. The sage mentions it as he opens his book so that the reader may be aroused to long for this high rung . . . the entire verse, then, is about the quest of the perfected person to attain this precious rung in the circle of the upright community. "Let Him kiss me" means "May He help me to cleave to Him!" speaking the language of those lovers who cling to one another in the intensity of their love and kiss with the kisses of their mouths.

While this exoteric commentary is formally Kabbalistic (it still makes mention of the sefirot), in Elisha Gallico's categories it should clearly be listed among the Neoplatonic, concerned as it is throughout with the individual soul and its longing to return to God. Rather obviously missing from Sahula's commentary is the national-collectivist allegory which had featured so prominently in the reading of the early sages. The "Community of Israel" has on the one hand been hypostatized to the point of inclusion within the deity, and on the other it has been atomized into an aggregate of individuals, each on a different rung in the striving for God. Lip service is paid here to "the circle of the upright community," but little more. Even in medieval Judaism, with all its deeply collectivist tendencies, the struggle for spiritual attainment was ultimately a lone one.

III

Finally we come to consideration of the Zohar itself. Suffice it to say, by way of introduction, that the Zohar makes all other users of Kabbalistic symbolism look like amateurs. Moses De Leon, in those years of inspiration when he wrote in the name of the ancient rabbi Simeon, raised the literary instrument of Kabbalah to dazzling new heights. His bold style is utterly enthralling; the reader is convinced that De Leon has succeeded in conveying within the language and style of the text itself something of the intensity of his own inner experience. Surely the language of the Zohar, which was to become an essential part of the vocabulary of Jewish spiritual expression for the next five centuries and beyond, has within it something of transcendence.

There is no consecutive commentary of the Zohar on the Song of Songs. The section of *Zohar Ḥadash* which begins to comment on the Song never goes beyond the first few verses. That text and the six-page section in volume two of the Zohar—a digression, as the Zohar comments, on the building of the tabernacle—form the most concentrated treatments. But the fact is that there exists hardly a page in the entire Zohar in which the Canticle is not in a broader sense discussed. Quotations from this relatively brief biblical book are everywhere, and even where it is not quoted, its theme remains central to the author's consciousness.

The Zohar takes the Solomonic superscription of the Song more seriously than had most prior Jewish commentators. While all agreed that Solomon was the author, we have already seen that the "true" origin of the Canticle was both higher and earlier; to those rabbis Solomon was presumably recorder or perhaps final editor of a text that had been passed down from the day it had been "given" until his generation. The name *Shlomo* had also, since early rabbinic times, been read supraliterally as "the king of peace," meaning God himself, and the rabbis had established that all references in the Song of Solomon, but for one, were to God.

Basing itself on a divergent rabbinic tradition, the Zohar asserts that the "day the Song was given" was in fact the day that Solomon completed his building of the Temple, and that there is an utter convergence between the King of Peace above and his earthly counterpart beneath.

> Rabbi Yosi opened with the verse: "The Song of Songs which is Solomon's." King Solomon composed this song when the Temple was built, when all the worlds, above and below, were perfected into a single wholeness. Even though the companions have some dispute about this, the Canticle was spoken only in this wholeness, when the moon was full and the Temple was built, just as it is above.
>
> From the day the world was created there was no hour of joy before God like that in which the Temple was erected. The tabernacle that Moses had put up in the desert in order to bring the *Shekhinah* down to earth—on the day it was erected another tabernacle went up above. Thus Scripture says *the* tabernacle was erected. *The* tabernacle refers to that other one that went up with it. This was the tabernacle of the angel Metatron, no more. But when the first Temple was erected, another first Temple was erected with it. It existed in all the worlds. Its light shone through them all and the cosmos was perfumed; all the upper windows were opened for the light to shine. There was no joy in all the worlds like the joy of that day. Then those above and those below proclaimed the song, and that is the "Song of Songs"—the song of those musicians who play before the blessed Holy One.
>
> King David composed "A Song of Ascents" and Solomon composed the "Song of Songs," the song of those musicians. What is the difference between them? They seem to be one, and indeed they are. But in the days of David the musicians had not yet taken their proper places, for the Temple was not yet built. . . . On the day the Temple was erected all of them were established in their places and the candle that had not

shone began to shine. The Song was created for the supreme
King, the King of peace; it is more exalted than any praise
which had yet existed. The day when that song of praise was
revealed in the world was a day of perfection throughout, and
that is why it *is* the Holy of Holies.

It was not out of special devotion to Solomon that the Zohar chose
to credit him so firmly with the Song. The Zohar was much involved
with its own reconstruction—on a purely theoretical and contemplative
plane—of Temple piety and the cult of sacrifice. This in turn has to do
with its tremendous emphasis on mythical cosmology and the vision of
cosmic wholeness. Its author saw himself living in a blemished universe,
one in which the full flow of Shekhinah's blessing into the world could
not be fully experienced. He longed frequently for the great time of
wholeness, that period when the smoke of the earthly altar would rise
into the heavens and arouse the altar in the Temple above, causing divine
radiance to shine throughout the cosmos and the world to be filled with
grace. Even the mystic, living as he does in an exiled cosmos, can have
but a taste of what all Israel had known fully in the days when the Temple
had stood. That the most perfect of songs should have been spoken on
that most perfect of days in the most perfect of places should not surprise
us when we hear it from the Zohar's author.

Still, this passage has gotten our author into a bit of trouble. He
seems to be placing Solomon on a higher level than Moses, the one who
is clearly "lord of all prophets" and whose encounter with God was never
to be equalled. Elsewhere in the Zohar, as throughout Jewish literature,
it is Moses who embodies the sublime vision, and the Zohar is sensitive
to the unspoken criticism. In prophecy, De Leon admits, Moses knows
no equal. But when it comes to the poetic muse, matters are somewhat
different. Moses' song—that of the sea—was still attached to matters of
this world; he was thanking God for Israel's deliverance and singing
praises of his miraculous deeds.

> But King David and his son Solomon spoke a different sort of
> Song. David sought to arrange the maidens and to adorn them
> along with the Queen, to show the Queen and her maidens in
> all their beauty. This is his concern in his Psalms and praises;
> it was they, Queen and maidens, he was seeking to adorn.
> When Solomon arrived he found the Queen adorned and her
> maidens decked out in beauty. He then sought to bring her to
> her bridegroom and to bring him under the canopy with his

bride. He spoke words of love between them so that they be joined as one, so that the two of them form a single one in the wholeness of love.

In this did Solomon rise high in praises above all other humans. Moses was wedded to the Queen in this world below so that there be a whole union among the lower creatures. Solomon brought about the complete union of the Queen above, first bringing the bridegroom under the canopy and only afterwards joyously inviting both of them into the Temple which he had built . . .

Blessed are David and Solomon his son for having brought about the union above. From the day God had said to the moon "Go and diminish yourself!" she had not been fully coupled with the sun until King Solomon came forth.

Moses the prophet still needs to bring the Shekhinah into the lower world. He has a people to worry about, a people wandering the wilderness who need assurance that God is indeed in their midst. The prophet's concern is his flock. Solomon, the mystic hierophant, can afford to be utterly selfless: it is not of his own love that he speaks, or even the love of earthly Israel for their God. He is the attendant, or perhaps the officiant, at the union of bridegroom and bride, offering his song as an epithalamium, a gift to the sacred couple, intending nothing more and nothing less than to fill all the universe with his freely given words of love. Here indeed the Song is cultic, in the full sense of the term. But now the cult is that of the mystic, in whose loving heart bride and bridegroom are joined as one.

Chronology

TEXTUAL		HISTORICAL
	?	The Creation and the Flood
	1800 B.C.E.	The Patriarchs and the Sojourn in Egypt (ca. 1800–1250)
	1700 B.C.E.	
	1600 B.C.E.	
	1500 B.C.E.	
	1400 B.C.E.	
	1300 B.C.E.	
	1200 B.C.E.	The Exodus and the Conquest (ca. 1250–1200)
		Joshua (ca. 1200–1150)
		The Judges (ca. 1150–1025)
	1100 B.C.E.	
		The Monarchy (ca. 1025–930)
The J Source (ca. 950–900)	1000 B.C.E.	
		The Two Kingdoms (ca. 930–590)

HISTORICAL

The Fall of Samaria (ca. 720)
The Reformation of Josiah (ca. 700–600)

The Fall of Jerusalem and the Exile to Babylonia
(ca. 587–538)

The Return (ca. 538)

Nehemiah and Ezra (ca. 475–350)

The Hellenistic Period (ca. 363–330)

900 B.C.E.

800 B.C.E.

700 B.C.E.

600 B.C.E.

500 B.C.E.

400 B.C.E.

TEXTUAL

The E Source (ca. 850–800)

Amos, Proverbs 10–22:16 (ca. 750)
Hosea (ca. 725)
Micah, Proverbs 25–29, Isaiah 1–31, JE redaction
(ca. 700)

Deuteronomy, Zephaniah (ca. 650)
Nahum, Proverbs 22:17–24 (ca. 625)
Deuteronomy-Kings (ca. 600–500), Jeremiah,
Habakkuk (ca. 600)
Job 3–31, 38–42:6 (ca. 575)
Isaiah 40–55, Job 32–37 (ca. 550)
Isaiah 56–66, Jeremiah 46–52, Ezekiel 1–37, 40–
48, Lamentations (ca. 525)
Job redaction, the P Source, Haggai, Zechariah
1–8, Jeremiah 30–31 (ca. 500)
Additions to Ezekiel 1–37, 40–48 (ca. 475–400)
Joel, Malachi, Proverbs 30–31, Lists (ca. 450)
JEP redaction [Genesis–Numbers], Isaiah 32–35,
Proverbs 1–9, Ruth, Obadiah (ca. 425)
JEPD redaction, Jonah, Psalms, Proverbs
redaction, Song of Songs, Chronicles, Ezra,
Nehemiah (ca. 400)
Ecclesiastes (ca. 350)

TEXTUAL		HISTORICAL
Zechariah 9–14 (ca. 325) Isaiah 24–27, Ezekiel 38–39 (ca. 300) The Septuagint, a translation of the Hebrew Bible into Greek (ca. 250–100)	300 B.C.E.	
	200 B.C.E.	
Daniel (ca. 175)		The Maccabean Revolt (ca. 165)
Esther (ca. 100)	100 B.C.E.	Pompey takes Jerusalem (ca. 63)
	10 B.C.E.	Birth of Christ (ca. 6)
	B.C.E. / C.E.	
	10 C.E.	
	20 C.E.	Baptism of Christ and the beginning of John's Ministry (ca. 26)
	30 C.E.	Crucifixion of Christ and Pentecost (ca. 30) Conversion of Paul (ca. 32)
	40 C.E.	Martyrdom of James (ca. 44) Paul and Barnabas visit Jerusalem during famine (ca. 46) Paul's First Missionary Journey (ca. 47–48) Paul's Second Missionary Journey (ca. 49–52)
Galatians (ca. 49) Thessalonian Letters (ca. 50)	50 C.E.	

TEXTUAL		HISTORICAL
		Paul's Third Missionary Journey (ca. 52–56)
Corinthian Letters (ca. 53–55)		Paul arrested in Jerusalem and imprisoned by Caesar (ca. 56–58)
Romans (ca. 56)		
Philippians (ca. 60)	60 C.E.	Paul's voyage to Rome and shipwreck (ca. 58)
Colossians, Philemon (ca. 61–62)		First Roman imprisonment of Paul (ca. 59–60)
Mark (ca. 65–67)		Paul's release and last travels (ca. 61–63)
		Paul's second Roman imprisonment and martyrdom (ca. 64–65)
		Death of Peter (ca. 64–65)
Matthew (ca. 75–80)	70 C.E.	Fall of Jerusalem (ca. 70)
Canonization of the Hebrew Bible at Synod of Jamnia (ca. 90)	80 C.E.	
	90 C.E.	Persecutions under Emperor Domitian discussed in Revelation (ca. 93–96)
Ephesians, Hebrews, Revelation, Luke, Acts (ca. 95); 1 Peter (ca. 95–100), Fourth Gospel (ca. 95–115)		
Johannine Epistles (ca. 110–115)	100 C.E.	
James, Jude (ca. 125–150)	125 C.E.	
2 Peter (ca. 150)	150 C.E.	
Timothy, Titus (ca. 160–175)		

HISTORICAL   TEXTUAL

200 C.E.

300 C.E.   Stabilization of the New Testament canon of twenty-seven books (ca. 350–400)

400 C.E.   Jerome completes the Latin Vulgate, a translation of the Bible based on the Septuagint and translated from the Hebrew (ca. 400)

500 C.E.

600 C.E.

700 C.E.

800 C.E.

900 C.E.

1000 C.E.

1100 C.E.

1200 C.E.

1300 C.E.

1400 C.E.   The first translation of the Bible into English, by John Wycliffe (ca. 1382)

1500 C.E.   The Gutenberg Bible printed from movable type, ushering in the new era of printing (1456)

Erasmus finishes a translation of the Bible into Greek (1516)

HISTORICAL

		1600 C.E.
		1700 C.E.
		1800 C.E.
		1900 C.E.

TEXTUAL

Martin Luther translates the Bible into German (1522)

William Tyndale's and Miles Coverdale's English translations of the Bible (1535)

Matthew's Bible produced, based on the Tyndale and Coverdale versions (1537)

The Great Bible produced by Coverdale (1539)

The Geneva Bible, the first to separate chapters into verses (1560)

The Douay-Rheims Bible, a Catholic translation from Latin into English (1582–1610)

The King James Version completed (1611)

The English Revised Version coissued by English and American scholars (1885)

The American Standard Version (1901)

The Moffatt Bible (1924)

The Smith-Goodspeed Bible (1931)

The Confraternity Version, an Episcopal revision of the Douay-Rheims Bible (1941)

Knox's Version, based on the Latin Vulgate and authorized by the Catholic Church (1945–49)

The Revised Standard Version (1952)

HISTORICAL

TEXTUAL

The New English Bible, Protestant (1961)
The Jerusalem Bible, Catholic (1966)
The Modern Language Bible (1969)
The New American Bible, Catholic (1970)
Today's English Version (1976)
The New International Version (1978)
The New Jewish Version (1982)

Contributors

HAROLD BLOOM, Sterling Professor of the Humanities at Yale University, is the author of *The Anxiety of Influence, Poetry and Repression,* and many other volumes of literary criticism. His forthcoming study, *Freud: Transference and Authority,* attempts a full-scale reading of all of Freud's major writings. A MacArthur Prize Fellow, he is the general editor of five series of literary criticism published by Chelsea House. In 1987–88, he served as Charles Eliot Norton Professor of Poetry at Harvard University.

WILLIAM E. PHIPPS is Professor of Religion and Philosophy at Davis and Elkins College in Elkins, West Virginia. He is the author of *The Sexuality of Jesus: Theological and Literary Perspectives* and other books.

MARVIN H. POPE was Professor of Near Eastern Languages and Literatures at Yale University until his retirement. He is the author of the Anchor Bible edition entitled *Song of Songs: A New Translation with Introduction and Commentary.*

PHYLLIS TRIBLE is Professor of the Old Testament at Union Theological Seminary in New York. Her best-known works are *God and the Rhetoric of Sexuality* and *Texts of Terror: Literary-Feminist Readings of Biblical Narratives.*

MARCIA FALK teaches in the Department of English at Pitzer College in Claremont, California. She was a Fulbright Scholar and is the author of *Love Lyrics from the Bible: A Translation and Literary Study of the Song of Songs.*

FRANCIS LANDY is Professor of Religious Studies at the University of Sussex. His work has appeared in numerous journals of biblical criticism. He is the author of *Paradoxes of Paradise: Identity and Difference in the Song of Songs.*

ROBERT ALTER is Professor of Comparative and Hebrew Literature at the University of California, Berkeley. His books include *The Art of Biblical Narrative* and *Defenses of the Imagination*.

ARTHUR GREEN is Acting President of the Reconstructionist Rabbinical College and Professor of Religious Studies at the University of Pennsylvania. He is the author of *Tormented Master: A Life of Rabbi Nahman of Bratslav*.

Bibliography

Cabaniss, Allen. "The Song of Songs in the New Testament." *Studies in English* 8 (1967): 53–56.

Carr, G. Lloyd. "Is the Song of Songs a Sacred Marriage Drama?" *Journal of the Evangelical Theological Society* 22 (1979): 103–14.

———. "The Old Testament Love Songs and Their Use in the New Testament." *Journal of the Evangelical Theological Society* 24 (1981): 97–105.

Chouraqui, André. "The Canticle of Solomon: An Introduction." *Service Inter. de Documentation Judeo-Chrétienne* 16 (1983): 4–7.

Cook, Albert S. *The Root of the Thing: A Study of Job and the Song of Songs.* Bloomington: Indiana University Press, 1969.

Cooper, Jerrold S. "New Cuneiform Parallels to the Song of Songs." *Journal of Biblical Literature* 90 (1971): 157–62.

Crim, Keith R. "'Your Neck Is Like the Tower of David': The Meaning of a Simile in the Song of Solomon 4.4." *The Bible Translator* 22 (1971): 70–74.

Exum, J. Cheryl. "A Literary and Structural Analysis of the Song of Songs." *Zeitschrift für die alttestamentliche Wissenschaft* 85 (1973): 47–79.

Falk, Marcia. *Love Lyrics from the Bible: A Translation and Literary Study of the Song of Songs.* Sheffield, England: Almond Press, 1982.

Fishbane, Michael. *Text and Texture: Close Readings of Selected Biblical Texts.* New York: Schocken, 1979.

Frye, Northrop. *The Great Code: The Bible and Literature.* New York and London: Harcourt Brace Jovanovich, 1982.

Gabel, John B., and Charles B. Wheeler. *The Bible as Literature—An Introduction.* Oxford: Oxford University Press, 1986.

Gollwitzer, Helmut. *Song of Love—A Biblical Understanding of Sex.* Translated by Keith Crim. Philadelphia: Fortress Press, 1979.

Good, Edwin M. "Ezekiel's Ship: Some Extended Metaphors in the Old Testament." *Semitics* 1 (1970): 79–103.

Gordis, Robert. "The Root DGL in the Song of Songs." *Journal of Biblical Literature* 88 (1969): 203–4.

———. *The Song of Songs and Lamentations: A Study, Modern Translation, and Commentary.* New York: KTAV, 1974.

Graves, Robert. *The Song of Songs: Text and Commentary.* London: Collins, 1973.

Greenspahn, Frederick E. "Words That Occur in the Bible Only Once—How Hard Are They to Translate?" *Bible Review* 1 (1985): 28–30.

Grober, S. F. "The Hospitable Lotus: A Cluster of Metaphors. An Inquiry into the Problem of Textual Unity in the Song of Songs." *Semitics* 9 (1984): 86–112.

Gros Louis, Kenneth R. R., and James S. Ackerman. *Literary Interpretations of Biblical Narratives.* Vol. 2. Nashville: Abingdon, 1982.

Habel, Norman. *Literary Criticism of the Old Testament.* Edited by J. Coert Rylaarsdam. Philadelphia: Fortress Press, 1971.

Jacobsen, T. *The Treasures of Darkness: A History of Mesopotamian Religion.* New Haven: Yale University Press, 1976.

Jay, Peter. *The Song of Songs.* Introduction by David Goldstein. London: Anvil, 1975.

Kramer, S. N. "The Sacred Marriage and Solomon's Song of Songs." In *The Sacred Marriage Rite: Aspects of Faith, Myth, and Ritual in Ancient Sumer.* Bloomington: Indiana University Press, 1969.

Kugel, James L. *The Idea of Biblical Poetry: Parallelism and Its History.* New Haven: Yale University Press, 1981.

Landy, Francis. *Paradoxes of Paradise: Identity and Difference in the Song of Songs.* Sheffield, England: Almond Press, 1983.

———. "The Song of Songs and the Garden of Eden." *Journal of Biblical Literature* 98 (1979): 513–28.

———. "Structure and Mythology in the Song of Songs." *Prospice* 11 (1981): 97–117.

Lee, J. M. "Song of Songs 5.10: My Beloved Is White and Ruddy." *Vetus Testamentum* 21 (1971): 609.

Lieberman, Saul. *"Mishnat Shir ha-Shirim."* In *Jewish Gnosticism, Merkabah Mysticism and Talmudic Tradition,* by Gershom Scholem, Appendix D. New York: Jewish Theological Seminary of America, 1960.

Maccoby, Hyam. "Sex According to the Song of Songs: Review of Marvin Pope's *The Song of Songs.*" *Commentary* 32, no. 6 (1979): 53–59.

Miskotte, Kornelis H. "Eros." In *When the Gods are Silent,* 264–71. London: Collins, 1967.

Murphy, Roland E. "Form-Critical Studies in the Song of Songs." *Interpretation* 27 (1973): 413–22.

———. "Interpreting the Song of Songs." *Biblical Theological Bulletin* 9 (1979): 99–105.

———. "Patristic and Medieval Exegesis: Help or Hindrance?" *The Catholic Bible Quarterly* 43 (1981): 505–16.

———. "Towards a Commentary on the Song of Songs." *Catholic Biblical Quarterly* 39 (1977): 482–96.

———. "The Unity of the Song of Songs." *Vetus Testamentum* 29 (1979): 436–43.

Pardee, Denys. "Review of Marvin H. Pope's *The Song of Songs.*" *Journal of Near Eastern Studies* 39 (1980): 79–82.

Patte, Daniel. "One Text: Several Structures." *Semeia* 18 (1980): 3–22.

Pope, Marvin H. "Response to Sasson on the Sublime Song." *Maarav* 2 (1980): 207–14.

———. *The Song of Songs.* Anchor Bible 7c. New York: Doubleday, 1977.

Rabin, Chaim. "The Song of Songs and Tamil Poetry." *Studies in Religion* 3 (1973): 205–19.

Raurell, Frederic. "Erotic Pleasure in the Song of Songs." *Laurentianum* 24 (1983): 5–45.

Rexroth, Kenneth. "Classics Revisited LXXXV: The Song of Songs." *Saturday Review of Literature* (26 April 1969): 16.

Robertson, David. *The Old Testament and the Literary Critic.* Edited by Gene M. Tucker. Philadelphia: Fortress Press, 1977.

Rowley, H. H. "The Interpretation of the Song of Songs." In *The Servant of the Lord and Other Essays,* 197–245. Oxford: Blackwell, 1965.

Sasson, Jack M. "A Further Cuneiform Parallel to the Song of Songs?" *Zeitschrift für die alttestamentliche Wissenschaft* 85 (1973): 359–60.

———. "On M. H. Pope's *Song of Songs.*" *Maarav* 1 (1979): 177–96.

———. "Unlocking the Poetry of Love in the Song of Songs." *Bible Review* 1 (1985): 10–19.

Schoville, Keith N. *The Impact of the Ras Shamra Tablets on the Study of the Song of Songs.* Ph.D. diss., University of Wisconsin, 1970.

———. "Song of Songs." *Encyclopaedia Judaica* 15 (1971): 143–50.

Segal, M. H. "The Song of Songs." *Vetus Testamentum* 12 (1962): 470–90.

Shea, William H. "The Chiastic Structure of the Song of Songs." *Zeitschrift für die alttestamentliche Wissenschaft* 92 (1980): 378–96.

Soulen, Richard N. "The *Wasfs* of the Song of Songs and Hermeneutic." *Journal of Biblical Literature* 86 (1967): 183–90.

Tournay, J-R. "The Song of Songs and Its Concluding Section." *Immanuel* 10 (1980): 5–14.

Trible, Phyllis. *God and the Rhetoric of Sexuality.* Philadelphia: Fortress Press, 1978.

Tucker, Gene M. *Form Criticism of the Old Testament.* Edited by J. Coert Rylaarsdam. Philadelphia: Fortress Press, 1971.

Ulanov, Barry. "The Song of Songs: The Rhetoric of Love." *The Bridge: A Yearbook* 4 (1962): 89–118.

Webster, Edwin. "Pattern in the Song of Songs." *Journal for the Study of the Old Testament* 22 (1982): 73–92.

White, John B. *A Study of the Language of Love in the Song of Songs and Ancient Egyptian Poetry.* Missoula, Mont.: Scholars Press for the Society of Biblical Literature, 1978.

Acknowledgments

"The Plight of the Song of Songs" by William E. Phipps from *Journal of the American Academy of Religion* 42, no. 1 (March 1974), © 1974 by the American Academy of Religion. Reprinted by permission.

"Interpretations of the Sublime Song: Love and Death" (originally entitled "Love and Death") by Marvin H. Pope from *The Anchor Bible: The Song of Songs: A New Translation with Introduction and Commentary,* edited and translated by Marvin H. Pope, © 1977 by Bantam, Doubleday Dell Publishing Group, Inc. Reprinted by permission of the publisher.

"Love's Lyrics Redeemed" by Phyllis Trible from *God and the Rhetoric of Sexuality* by Phyllis Trible, © 1978 by Fortress Press. Reprinted by permission of the publisher.

"The *Waṣf*" by Marcia Falk from *Love Lyrics from the Bible: A Translation and Literary Study of the Song of Songs,* edited by David M. Gunn, © 1982 by the Almond Press. Reprinted by permission.

"Beauty and the Enigma" by Francis Landy from *Paradoxes of Paradise: Identity and Difference in the Song of Songs,* edited by David M. Gunn, © 1983 by the Almond Press.

"The Garden of Metaphor" by Robert Alter from *The Art of Biblical Poetry* by Robert Alter, © 1985 by Robert Alter. Reprinted by permission of the author and Basic Books, Inc., publishers.

"The Song of Songs in Early Jewish Mysticism" by Arthur Green from *Orim* 2, no. 2 (Spring 1987), © 1987 by Arthur Green. Reprinted by permission of the author.

Index